1967

1967

Chris Amon, Scuderia Ferrari and a year of **living dangerously**

John Julian

Foreword by Jonathan Williams, and contributions from Chris Amon, John Surtees, Dan Gurney, Roger Bailey, Annabel Parkes Campigotto, Howden Ganley, David Hobbs, Jackie Oliver, Eva Marie Saint, and Brenda Vernor

ISBN: 978 1 935007 24 1

Design and production: Punaromia Publications/PressGang, www.pressgang.co.nz
Printed in China

10 9 8 7 6 5 4 3 2 1

Published in the United States and United Kingdom by

David Bull Publishing
4250 East Camelback Road, Suite K150
Phoenix, AZ 85018

602-852-9500
602-852-9503 (fax)

www.bullpublishing.com

First published as a Limited Edition by Auckland Maritime Projects Ltd, New Zealand, 2013

This edition published by David Bateman Ltd, 2013
30 Tarndale Grove, Albany, Auckland, New Zealand, www.batemanpublishing.co.nz

Contents

Dedication

NICK LOUDON

For Chris Amon
on the occasion of his
seventieth birthday,
20 July 2013

'Believe me! The secret of reaping the greatest fruitfulness and the greatest enjoyment from life is to *live dangerously!*'
– Friedrich Nietzsche

'There are only three sports: bullfighting, motor racing and mountaineering; all the rest are merely games.'
– Ernest Hemingway

THE KLEMANTASKI COLLECTION

ABOVE
Monaco, 1967: Chris Amon (Ferrari V12) leads Mike Spence (BRM H16) towards the old Tabac Corner. Spence would finish sixth, three places behind Amon.

'The danger? Well, of course. But you are missing a very important point. I think if any of us imagined — really imagined — what it would be like to go into a tree at 150 miles per hour we would probably never get into the cars at all, none of us. So it has always seemed to me that to do something very dangerous requires a certain absence of imagination.'
– Manetta-Ferrari (see Appendix 2A) driver Jean-Pierre Sarti (Yves Montand) talking to Louise Frederickson (Eva Marie Saint) during John Frankenheimer's 1966 movie *Grand Prix*. No other film has brought the viewer closer to Formula One motor racing, its key players, and the spirit of the sport itself, and the reasons why men risk their lives in order to compete.

GRAND PRIX PHOTO

Foreword

I am delighted to have been asked to write the Foreword to this book by John Julian, which describes Chris Amon's first year at Ferrari. I had already been at Maranello for a couple of months before Chris arrived. We had not previously met, but I knew about him, that he had won the 24 hours of Le Mans with fellow Kiwi Bruce McLaren, that he was fast. When we did meet, it was a pleasure to discover that he was no prima donna, just relaxed, open and friendly, an easy person to like.

The weather at that time of year was bad; fog could last for weeks at a time, fuelled by the mighty river Po. It could become depressing so, when we had no testing commitment, we would 'borrow' a Ferrari in the morning and head south up into the Apennines on the winding road to Lucca, and after a few kilometres of climbing break out into bright sunshine, a sea of vapour below, with the Alps in the far distance. Our destination was a bar in the small town of Serramazzoni where I introduced Chris to the local habit of having a grappa with one's coffee, something Mike Parkes had taught me. Sometimes Mike came too, but he had a day job as chief engineer for the production cars which limited his free time. When lunchtime approached, we would descend back into the gloom and head for the Cavallino restaurant.

Chris got on very well with Mauro Forghieri; there was a lot of mutual respect there, and with all the mechanics despite his limited vocabulary in Italian. They appreciated the fact he liked their food and drank the local purple-coloured Lambrusco wine. I think that Chris's Italian at that time consisted of *buongiorno*, *cappuccino*, *grazie*, and *Malaguti*, this last being the name of the constructor of small motor scooters, of which we each had one for nipping about Modena. He liked to practise saying this word under his breath after having drunk a few glasses of Lambrusco. It is my belief he also had a special rapport with Enzo Ferrari. Drivers were just employees to the Commendatore, but once in a while he saw something he liked: natural talent, bravery, we will never know. Gilles Villeneuve was another driver he favoured.

1967 was a terrible year at Ferrari. Lorenzo Bandini succumbed to the injuries he received at Monaco, Günter Klass died instantly on hitting a tree at Mugello, and Mike Parkes broke both his legs after losing control at Spa on oil spilled from Jackie Stewart's BRM. Ludovico Scarfiotti took time out to think things over only to die the following spring while driving a Porsche in a hill climb. This left only me and Chris standing, so, by default, I became part of the Can-Am team. I was more than happy to go to California for the first time, even though I knew I would be trashed on the track by Chris, and so it was. It helps to race a Maserati 250F when you are 18. Everyone should do it. We moved on to Mexico for the Formula One race where, to my surprise, halfway through the last practice session I was bundled into the spare car, propped up with foam rubber and told to get on with it. Records show that I beat Chris in the race, but he ran out of fuel while fighting at the front and I didn't while fighting at the back. Historians beware! I lost my chance of continuing to enjoy his company in 1968 after I knocked all four wheels off an F1 car during an autumn test at Modena. Such is life.

Today people still argue about why a driver of Chris's talent didn't win a championship race or, indeed, become World Champion. There are two popular theories, the first being that he partied too hard with Mike Hailwood. Rubbish. In those days I don't think many drivers had seen the inside of a gym, and most of the single ones spent their free time chasing women.

The other theory is that he was too nice a guy. No argument about being nice, but in a car Chris had as much steel as anyone else on the track.

The truth can be found in one word: timing. If he had stayed another year at Ferrari, he would have been driving Mauro Forghieri's masterpiece, and Formula One history would be different. Instead he went to March where the management broke every promise they had made to him, then to Matra where the car failed to deliver and then he built his own F1 car, ahead of its time, but which even Chris's consummate skills as a test driver failed to tame.

In an interview with Simon Taylor, Chris said he had no regrets, preferring to be alive and active, than to be a dead ex World Champion. It's hard to disagree with that.

Jonathan Williams

OPPOSITE
Chris Amon and Jonathan Williams during testing at Monza, early 1967.

Author's note

'If you can meet with triumph and disaster
And treat those two impostors just the same.'

– Rudyard Kipling: 'If—', *Rewards and Fairies,* 1910

1967 is a book I have wanted to write for some time, but it was not until July 2011 that I telephoned Chris Amon to ask whether he had any objection to the idea. He did not and, furthermore, he has encouraged me from the outset and been immensely generous with his time, advice, memories and contacts. The fact that Jonathan Williams, his only remaining Grand Prix teammate from that year, not only volunteered to write the Foreword but also introduced me to several of his friends, while also patiently explaining details of life at Ferrari during the course of what would prove to be an exceedingly taxing year, was a tremendous bonus. I am very grateful to them both.

I am also indebted to Nigel Roebuck and Eoin Young, masters of motor racing narrative, who have sustained my interest in the sport since boyhood and some of whose works I have quoted from here. The same goes for Gerald Donaldson, Maurice Hamilton, Alan Henry and Peter Windsor, and I would urge those who may not have read their books and articles to do so. I also owe many thanks to the late Richard Garrett, whose books *Fast and Furious* (1968) and *Anatomy of a Grand Prix Driver* (1970) are authentic and interesting accounts of those days.

The purpose of *1967* is in some ways similar to that of books written about the air war of 1939–45 and, more particularly, the Battle of Britain in 1940. It is intended to give younger readers a glimpse of Grand Prix motor racing in the late 1960s at a time when a driver's life expectancy wasn't much greater than that of a wartime fighter pilot and many of the hazards, most notably death or serious injury, frequently by fire, applied to both disciplines. I lived across the street from a Battle of Britain pilot for some years, a wonderful man named Paddy Barthropp, who had moved to Hampshire with his wife Betty, a lovely, funny, British beauty. He used to take me to air shows and reunions and, with him, I met other men who had flown powerful fighter aircraft in combat.

I used to watch them greet each other and while most were close friends of many years' standing, there was still a lightness of touch; perhaps a moment's wry, self-deprecating humour along with a mild reluctance to display too much affection, just in case they were meeting for the last time; that one or more of them might be missing the following day. I've seen it among the older drivers too, men who competed in those different and dangerous days and survived, but who couldn't look their wives or girlfriends in the eye at the time and say that they would definitely be back for supper that evening. And so it was for Paddy during the late summer and early autumn of 1940 … drinks tonight at the White Hart at Brasted and flying from Biggin Hill in the morning, but tomorrow evening: who knew where any of them might be — dead or alive, hurt or unscathed, imprisoned or on the run? Nobody knew.

It is quite unthinkable, 46 years on, that the 1967 race at Monaco would be allowed to continue until the finish, opposite the Royal Box 18 laps later, with drivers darting through a narrow gap between Lorenzo Bandini's capsized and blazing Ferrari, along with those attempting to extinguish the flames and free him from the wreckage, and the barrier on the landward side of the section of street circuit surrounding the port. Bandini later died at the Princess Grace Polyclinic in Monte Carlo from the third-degree burns he sustained to more than 70 per cent of his body when the car caught fire, and over 100,000 people attended his funeral later that week in the Italian town of Reggiolo, north of Modena, off the A22 to Verona.

1967 is also for older people who can remember those days before the advent of laptop computers and mobile telephones, safety harnesses and full-face helmets, self-sealing fuel cells and on-board fire extinguishers, pit to cockpit communications, anti-lock braking, semi-automatic gearboxes and traction control, among other things. It is about some of the most beautiful cars ever to compete in Grand Prix motor racing during that last season before the appearance of wings and large advertising logos; most notably the Eagle Gurney-Weslake V12 and the Ferrari 312/67 V12, the Honda RA300 V12 and the Lotus 49-Cosworth V8. And it is about hotels like the Metropole in Monte Carlo and the Villa d'Este near Lake Como, parties in palaces and dinners on yachts, a feeling of family and a sense of the circus, with a constant, nagging reminder that the spectre of death or serious injury for driver or onlooker, marshal or medic might only be a lap away.

Readers of all age groups with a good knowledge of Grand Prix racing at the time will recognise names and places, cars and teams. I have introduced different narrators, invented some conversations and staged some encounters in the spirit and the style of those days. This is not intended to mislead; it is just that some of the characters I was fortunate enough to know are no longer with us so I can't ask them whether they did, for instance, have supper at the Green Man in Syresham, near Silverstone during the weekend of the 1967 British Grand Prix or whether they dined in Brackley, Stony Stratford, Towcester or elsewhere. Furthermore, there are a few examples of overlap where the narrative strays, either backwards into 1966 or forward into 1968. All quotations are attributed and, as far as the racing goes, I have conjured up nothing but the truth and I obviously accept full responsibility for any errors.

Perhaps the best thing about *1967* from a writer's point of view is that everybody I got in touch with wanted to be involved with the book and nobody I spoke with had anything but happy memories of times spent racing or relaxing with Chris, be they rival or teammate, friend or fan. That was a much greater compliment than I could pay this brave, accomplished, modest and generous man for it is difficult to think of many long-standing Grand Prix drivers or top sportsmen of any stripe who still enjoy the universal and unqualified respect and affection of their peers, not to mention the media, after all this time. Thank you Chris and thank you Jonathan for taking me along for the ride as you recalled the events of nearly 50 years ago.

John Julian

NICK LOUDON

'It's almost time to go. The cars are on the grid in eight rows of two and some drivers are already in their cockpits, but you prefer to stay out of yours until a few minutes before the off in case you get cramp in your calves or the muscles of your thighs convulse and your legs start twitching. You squeeze your spongy wax earplugs into place and roll your face mask over your chin and up to the bridge of your nose, looking skyward now, through the trees, to avoid eye contact with the journalists and photographers and the masses of other people still wandering round looking at the cars and the mechanics making final adjustments to them and you see heavy grey clouds advancing in the direction of the harbour from the hills to the north. It rained earlier and more is forecast for later. Parts of the circuit are still damp.'

– John Julian

CHAPTER 1

Modena and Maranello, spring

ACCOMPANIMENT: 'Nessun Dorma', an aria from the final act of Giacomo Puccini's opera *Turandot* performed by Luciano Pavarotti, born in Modena 12 October 1935, died in Modena 6 September 2007.

There are knights in Italy and, as in other parts of the world, they fall into various categories. Some Italian knighthoods are awarded for religious reasons and others for political or business distinction. The City of Modena was once home to two particularly prominent Knights of Industry, Enzo Ferrari and Giorgio Fini. By 1967, the former was well known internationally as the founder of the eponymous road and racing car concern, while the latter owned the Real-Fini Hotel, across the road from Ferrari's home, and produced some of the region's best-known foods, including Modena's celebrated balsamic vinegar.

Anyone enjoying breakfast at the Real-Fini during the last few days of April might have seen a well-dressed young man drinking coffee and reading the paper before setting off for work. He never seemed unduly hurried and something about his spare, athletic frame suggested he was not about to spend the day sitting behind a desk. Quite a number of people seemed to know him including the hotel barber, who shaved him every morning. But it was as clear from the young man's complexion as it was from his conversations with the barber that he wasn't Italian. So where had he come from and what was he doing in Modena?

Chris Amon had originally come from New Zealand and was a knight of a different kind: a works Ferrari driver whose cars carried the emblem of Il Cavallino Rampante or The Prancing Horse. This tradition began on 17 June 1923 when Enzo Ferrari won a motor race in Ravenna and was introduced to the Countess Paolina, mother of the First World War air ace Count Francesco Baracca. She presented him with the crest that had adorned her son's aircraft; suggesting it might bring him good luck, and racing Ferraris carry a modified version of that heraldic symbol to this day. History was important to Chris, which was one of the reasons for the shaving ritual, for his barber used to lather the face of Tazio Nuvolari, the celebrated Alfa Romeo and Maserati driver of the 1930s. Chris, aged 23 in early 1967, was already in very good company!

THE JONATHAN WILLIAMS COLLECTION

Chris Amon and Jonathan Williams look through the 1967 Ferrari Year Book during a reception at the Hotel Real-Fini in Modena.

'Chris was and, for many of us, remains to this day the best test driver Ferrari ever had and everyone agrees on this. It's probably why the Old Man engaged him, apart from the fact that he was also a quick driver.'

– Brenda Vernor to John Julian, September 2012

In spite of his relative youth, however, Enzo Ferrari's new driver had four seasons of Formula One racing and victory in the 1966 Le Mans 24 Hour Race to his credit, but his route to the top had been unconventional. He was testing a Maserati 250F aged 17 and racing it at 18, and he so impressed those members of the international Formula One fraternity, who were visiting New Zealand to contest the 1962–63 Tasman Series during the southern hemisphere summer, that he was invited to join the Parnell Grand Prix team (see Appendix 2B) with almost immediate effect. He flew to England just in time to race a T4 Lola-Climax at Goodwood on Easter Monday 1963. 'I finished fifth,' he remembered later. 'It was the first Formula One race I had seen and I was in it!'

Chris would go on to compete in a variety of Lola and Lotus cars with Climax and BRM engines, starting his first Grand Prix at Spa Francorchamps on 9 June 1963 at the age of 19 years and 324 days (the youngest ever to do so at the time, and for some years to come) and scoring his first World Championship points at the Dutch Grand Prix on 24 May 1964. However, Reg Parnell's untimely death in January of that year would hit the team hard and, by 1965, Chris was working with fellow New Zealander Bruce McLaren and racing the latter's five-litre McLaren-Elva Mk II V8 sports cars while becoming an ever more accomplished test driver, most notably for Firestone, who engaged McLaren Cars to evaluate and improve their tyres. This meant that Chris sometimes completed up to 1000 miles per week during testing in cars that were at least as powerful as the three-litre Grand Prix machines due to replace the 1500 cc examples at the beginning of 1966.

A planned season of Grand Prix racing with McLaren in 1966 was abandoned due to difficulty with engine supply, so Bruce and Chris concentrated on sports cars, both in America, where they contested Can-Am races, finishing third and sixth overall in their McLaren M1Bs, and Europe, where they won Le Mans for Ford on 19 June and helped John Frankenheimer make his epic Cinerama movie *Grand Prix* at various circuits, including Monaco, Clermont-Ferrand, Spa, Brands Hatch and Monza, with Chris doing much of the driving in the Ford GT40 camera car. This endeavour won him new fans from different backgrounds including the actor James Garner, a very competent driver himself, and Eva Marie Saint, the movie's leading lady, who told John Julian in 2011 that 'at some point I began to focus on the talent and bravery of the drivers and, to this day, I have such respect for Chris Amon and all his buddies!' Chris also contested the French Grand Prix at Reims in a Cooper-Maserati on 3 July but, in most respects, it was an unconventional year for an established Formula One driver.

The United States Grand Prix was at Watkins Glen in upstate New York on 2 October that year and Chris went to watch it between Can-Am commitments at Mosport Park and Laguna Seca. Ferrari had a habit of making indirect approaches to potential drivers through sponsors and suppliers, trusted agents and intermediaries and so it was that Keith Ballisat of Shell cornered Chris in the Glen Motor Inn and asked him whether he was free to make a trip to Italy before his next North American race.

THE CAHIER ARCHIVE

THE CAHIER ARCHIVE

ABOVE
The Ford Mark II in which Chris Amon and Bruce McLaren won the 24 Hours of Le Mans on 19 June 1966.

LEFT
Chris (left) and Bruce (right) discuss Le Mans strategy with Carroll Shelby, whose company Shelby American managed the racing programme for the Ford Motor Company.

'The whole [contract signing] thing took about ten minutes. There wasn't much talk about money, just a standard retainer. Then we went to the Cavallino for lunch. I was on my best behaviour, drinking water, and Ferrari said, "When Mike Hawthorn signed for me, we came here for lunch and he drank half a bottle of my best malt whisky!"'

– Chris Amon to Simon Taylor of *Motor Sport*, 2008

WIKIPEDIA

Enzo Anselmo Ferrari: born in Modena on 18 February 1898 and died in Modena on 14 August 1988. His legacy transcends the art and science of road and racing car production.

'Would you like to come to Maranello with me and meet Mr Ferrari?' asked the Shell man, whose company had been involved with Ferrari since the very beginning. 'It took me about two seconds to say "Yes",' recalled Chris later, 'but actually I was in a difficult situation. Bruce wanted me to stay at McLaren but driving for Ferrari was also a boyhood ambition of mine — I'd sort of loved Ferraris from the time I got interested in racing.'

By the end of 1966, *Commendatore* (or Knight Commander) Enzo Ferrari was 68, powerful and autocratic, determined and uncompromising, a man who had built some of the fastest and most beautiful racing cars in the world and had employed the best men he could find to drive them. He had also produced some of the most strikingly handsome road cars too, although the pleasure he took in their appearance and performance was tempered by his feelings towards those who willingly paid as much as they did to buy them. There was one thing, though … expensive as they were, they generated more revenue to spend on racing!

That, of course, had been a great success, both in single-seaters and sports cars. Foremost among a myriad of honours, Formula One drivers' titles had been won in Ferraris by Alberto Ascari (1952–53), Juan Manuel Fangio (1956), Mike Hawthorn (1958), Phil Hill (1961) and John Surtees (1964) before Chris arrived, and the magnificent sequence of Le Mans victories (including six consecutive wins between 1960 and 1965) was itself broken by Chris with Bruce McLaren in the Ford Mk II.

Chris arrived in Modena in late October and made the short trip out to the Ferrari factory at Maranello with mixed feelings. 'I was absolutely in awe of Enzo Ferrari,' he told Simon Taylor of *Motor Sport* in 2008. 'I asked him about Formula One and he said, "Do you want to drive for me or not? I know you have Formula One ambitions, but I'm not going to put it in your contract." I signed anyway. The whole thing took about ten minutes. There wasn't much talk about money, just a standard retainer. Then we went to the Cavallino for lunch. I was on my best behaviour, drinking water, and Ferrari said, "When Mike Hawthorn signed for me, we came here for lunch and he drank half a bottle of my best malt whisky!"'

And so there were four Ferrari Formula One drivers, including Chris, under contract for 1967. Lorenzo Bandini, the 31 year old from Milan with 41 Grands Prix to his credit, all but seven of which he had contested in Ferraris, had been born in Libya but his family returned to Italy in 1939. He went to work as a mechanic in Milan and started racing cars in 1957 with the support of his employer and future father-in-law Goliardo Freddi (whose daughter Margherita Lorenzo would marry in 1963) and competed in his first Grand Prix at Spa in 1961. Mike Parkes, a 35-year-old Englishman, was an automotive engineer who raced sports Ferraris with Willy Mairesse, Umberto Maglioli, Jean Guichet and John Surtees before moving up to Formula One after Surtees' departure and scoring two second places in four Grand Prix starts before the end of 1966.

The fourth driver was Ludovico Scarfiotti, the 33-year-old all-rounder who had won Le Mans with Lorenzo Bandini in 1963 and who, like Bandini, had also won a Grand Prix for Ferrari. His Formula One victory, however, had been celebrated just the month before on 4 September 1966, when he had beaten Mike Parkes into second place during the Italian Grand Prix at Monza. He was the first Italian to win the home race in 15 years and the 1–2 result earned both drivers a rapturous reception from the proudly partisan crowd that packs the Autodromo every year. Formerly a royal park, Monza remains the most atmospheric of circuits and one of the few to retain its original, albeit presently disused, banked track like Montlhéry, close to Paris, or the semi-derelict Brooklands near Weybridge, outside London.

'We all went to Daytona for a week in December to test the new P4 sports car. I realised I had to get on the pace pretty quick if I wanted a Formula One seat. Lorenzo was very fast, so it was between the three of us. Fortunately, my times were about the same as Bandini's,' recalled Chris Amon later. The P4 would go on to win the 24-hour race at Daytona and the Monza 1000 km in April with Chris and Lorenzo at the helm on both occasions and the wins would result in an exquisite, V12-engined Ferrari grand touring car being named the Daytona. Sadly, they would also be the last victories of Lorenzo Bandini's all-too-short life before he died as a result of a fiery accident on the eighty-second lap of the Monaco Grand Prix on 7 May 1967.

That Monaco race was Chris's first World Championship Grand Prix as a Ferrari driver and he finished third, behind Denny Hulme (the New Zealander who would become World Champion that year) and Graham Hill, who would win five times at Monaco during a long and illustrious career. Chris had spent a day with Lorenzo the week before and they had subsequently driven to Monaco together and the young New Zealander had found his teammate in a philosophical frame of mind. Many years later, Chris related this to Nigel Roebuck in a passage that appeared in the latter's excellent book, *Chasing the Title*:

'I was never a great one for believing in premonitions, but the Wednesday before the race at Monaco made me wonder. We went off for lunch in the mountains and, on the drive back, Lorenzo seemed very reflective, very aware of the simple things in life – you know, flowers, the fact that it was spring, and so on. On the way down, he saw an old man fishing by the side of the road and he stopped, just to watch him quietly for a while. It's difficult to convey what I'm getting at, but it was almost as if he were savouring life, as if he knew something was going to happen. I'll never forget that day.'

'As this book title says they were all "living dangerously". They worked hard and played hard. ... I think the drivers were all very aware of the Grim Reaper stalking in the background but preferred not to think about it.'
– Annabel Parkes Campigotto to John Julian, October 2012

Modena memories

by Annabel Parkes

'In 1967 I was working in Milan as a market researcher for McCann Erickson, the advertising agency, so it was quite easy for me to drive down to Modena to see Mike at weekends. In reality this did not happen all that often because Mike lived a very hectic life between his work as a development engineer on the Ferrari production cars and racing in Italy and abroad. If you look at the race list on www.mikeparkes.eu, you can see where he went. After his accident at Spa in June he spent most of the rest of the year in England, much of it in hospital.

'Life in Modena was very different from the glamour of the racetracks. It was a smallish provincial town where everybody knew everybody else. Mike used to go to the barber where Ferrari had a shave every morning and catch up on the local gossip. Often at the bar of the Hotel Fini you could run into drivers or other people involved in racing. Mike really liked the atmosphere and human warmth of Modena and kept his flat there even after moving to Turin to work at Lancia.

'Being a bachelor, Mike never ate at home and we often went to dinner at Luigi's, a small traditional restaurant where he was a regular customer. Luigi, who was quite portly and in his fifties, would appear from the kitchen to take our order with his glasses perched halfway down his nose. The waiter knew without being told that at the end of dinner he had to provide an ice cream on a plate on the floor for Mike's Labrador Fred. Another place where we went to eat was the restaurant opposite the Ferrari factory gate where Ferrari took his guests and many of the drivers went. There was always a lot of banter and gossip.

'Sometimes, when Mike had to do a road test on a production car, I would go with him on a spin up into the Apennines. The cars were usually prototypes and pretty uncomfortable with lots of exposed metal and none of the finishes inside. One time he was stopped for speeding. In those days there were no speed cameras and the police would simply park a patrol car by the side of the road just round a bend and then jump on unwary motorists with a "lollipop" palette and accuse them of speeding. For Mike this was a challenge. First he pretended not to speak Italian. Then, when the police asked him to pay an on-the-spot fine, he started producing foreign currency: dollars, sterling, francs, anything but lira. Faced with the problem of doing a currency conversion the police gave up and let him off. I don't think he really cared that much about the money; it was just the fun of cocking a snook at authority. Another time, he solemnly explained to the policemen that it was very difficult to make a Ferrari go slowly and they laughed and let him off.

'In general, although not aggressive in manner, Mike was very competitive. One time in the winter we were driving up the snow-covered Maloja Pass in a Ferrari to San Moritz, when we were overtaken by an Alfa Romeo. This was like a red rag to a bull. Mike overtook the Alfa Romeo and tore off up the hairpin bends with the Alfa Romeo in pursuit. After a while we heard crashing noises behind us and no more was seen of the Alfa Romeo. I think most of the drivers of that era were up for any road race. No worries about being splashed all over the tabloids for misbehaviour.

'The driver I met most often was Ludovico Scarfiotti, who was one of Mike's closest friends. They used to fool around a lot together, playing jokes on each other. Quite a lot of Mike's spare time was spent flying. He qualified for his pilot's licence in February 1967 and shortly afterwards acquired a share in a Beechcraft Baron. From April onwards he started using it to fly to races (at Silverstone, Siracusa, Zandvoort, Le Mans and Spa).

'The whole atmosphere of the racing scene was totally different from today. I remember going several times to dinner at a hotel in Arcore after races at Monza. A lot of the drivers, from different teams, who had been competing against each other in the afternoon, would meet up in the evening to eat and joke together. There was no question of not being able to talk to people from other teams for reasons of security. I am told that nowadays everyone flies off immediately after the race.

'As this book title says they were all "living dangerously". They worked hard and played hard. Although the amount Mike earned was modest compared with today's F1 stars it was enough to have a good time and, not having any family responsibilities, he wasn't worrying about saving up for his old age. Better to spend it on going out for nice meals and flying. I think the drivers were all very aware of the Grim Reaper stalking in the background but preferred not to think about it.'

– Annabel Parkes Campigotto (Michael Parkes' sister and author of the encyclopaedic website www.mikeparkes.eu) to John Julian, October 2012

There is no doubt that Chris's easy self-confidence was as natural as his abundant talent, and these virtues were valued by his Italian employer and his own countrymen, as was his tendency towards self-deprecation and articulate understatement. He would need all these qualities in large measure during the year to come. Chris had arrived in Italy and signed a contract with the most powerful and charismatic team owner in Grand Prix motor racing history without so much as a lawyer or manager present. He was then dispatched to a circuit in the United States which, admittedly, he knew well and won a place in Ferrari's Formula One team alongside three incumbent drivers.

'There is no doubt that Chris's easy self-confidence was as natural as his abundant talent, and these virtues were valued by his Italian employer and his own countrymen, as was his tendency towards self-deprecation and articulate understatement. He would need all these qualities in large measure during the year to come.'

New Zealanders tend to give of their best in an uphill struggle, but they don't talk it up too much, either prior to the event or later on. Sir Ed Hillary was inclined to make the ascent of Everest sound fairly straightforward although he advocated maximum respect for the elements, just as Sir Peter Blake did later as he raced yachts round the world, and Chris remains modest about his many motor sporting achievements to this day. Bruce McLaren and Denny Hulme were Grand Prix front-runners as well during 1967, with the latter winning the World Championship in a Repco-powered Brabham BT24. New Zealand drivers' stock had never been higher.

While victories in the sports cars at Daytona and at Monza were behind Chris, Monaco was on his mind as he strolled out of the Real-Fini on that late April morning and got into the modest Fiat saloon he used from day to day. He would drive the 20-odd kilometres to Maranello and make his way up to Enzo Ferrari's office. There, he would talk over the day's arrangements and any forthcoming travel plans with Valerio Stradi, the Commendatore's secretary, a haunted man known as 'Ferrari's scratching post' because of the lacerating treatment he received on a daily basis. And then he would call on Mauro Forghieri, Chief of the Technical Department for Racing Cars, to review notes from the last *collaudo*, or testing session, and discuss the schedule for that afternoon. Soon it would be time for *tortellini* and a tomato salad at the Cavallino with *acqua minerale* to drink and *caffe* to finish before heading back to town and on to the Aerautodromo di Modena, where a svelte, scarlet single-seater with golden wheels, a three-litre V12 engine and a white, Medusa-like tangle of exhaust pipes between the cylinder heads would be warmed and waiting for him in the pits, the mechanics busy changing plugs, taking tyre pressures or checking the roll bar or spring settings.

There Chris would change into flame-resistant white overalls, made by Hinchman and adorned with the logos of Firestone and Shell with red stripes running down either arm. He would grip the sides of his red, white and blue Bell helmet where the straps are attached to the hard outer shell and ease it over his head, passing the webbing tongue through the D-rings and pulling it tight. And then he would reach for the goggles hanging round his neck and work them upwards over his eyes and under the white peak of the helmet with the elastic stretched around the back of it before pulling on his Les Leston Protex gloves and stepping into the car.

Supporting himself on the cockpit sides, he would then slide his legs under the leather-bound steering wheel with the Ferrari badge at its centre, easing them into the footwell, raising his arms as he did so and shrugging his shoulders as he brought his gloved hands forward and then down. Then Giulio Borsari the chief mechanic would lean over the cockpit and murmur a few last words and Chris would reach up and cuff him on the arm. They would grin at one another before the driver returned to the starting sequence and the mechanic stepped back from the car, and there would be a harsh bark followed by a crackling roar and a joyful howl as 312/67 V12/0003 came to life. It would be the last test before the 1967 Monaco Grand Prix, where different trials awaited the young man on that venerable street circuit.

THE CAHIER ARCHIVE

'The sixties have turned out to be a good decade thus far for a single, successful racing driver and you have enjoyed your share of the long-haired, kohl-eyed, high-heeled, mini-skirted dolly birds that have become a part of the largely English-speaking Grand Prix scene. But this girl is different, both French and fatalistic, more Françoise Hardy than Brigitte Bardot, most at home aboard her houseboat on the Seine in Paris with her books, and it pains you to picture her writing up your lap chart and fretting when you are racing and therefore too busy to think about her.'

– John Julian

CHAPTER 2

Cars and drivers

ACCOMPANIMENT: Soundtrack music by Maurice Jarre from Metro-Goldwyn-Mayer's 1966 movie *Grand Prix*: 'Sarti and Louise Fishing' [4:02] and 'The Clermont Ferrand Race' [2:18].

'I thought that, for 1967, Ferrari had the confidence to turn the tables on BRM, Maserati, Repco and, later, Cosworth and that there was enough in the pipeline mechanically for that to happen, and that they had a couple of potential World Champions.'

– John Surtees to John Julian, January 2013

1967 was the second year of the three-litre Formula One car rule and Ferrari chose to run two Grand Prix machines for a four-man squad, which consisted of Chris Amon, Lorenzo Bandini, Mike Parkes and Ludovico Scarfiotti. This arrangement was designed to hone the drivers' competitive edge and to foster creative tension between them. They also vied for supremacy in the beautiful 330 P4 sports cars with Pedro Rodriguez and Jean Guichet also racing a NART Ferrari 412P, effectively a P3/P4 for privateers. Paul Frère, a distinguished Belgian journalist and former Ferrari Grand Prix driver, who also won Le Mans for the marque in 1960 with his countryman Olivier Gendebien, wrote about this practice in the November 1968 edition of *Sports Car Graphic*.

'It is often said that letting the team drivers find out for themselves who is faster is the quickest way to get them killed, and that Ferrari just doesn't care. It is certainly true that drivers who must really fight for their living will tend to take more risks — but, after all, to beat the opposition is the essence of any sport. Ferrari will always forgive a man for going off the road and wrecking a car if there has been a real reason for trying hard, and he will give him a chance again and again. But the sort of driver who never puts a wheel wrong, just because he keeps a reasonable safety margin, does not usually get old as a Ferrari team member. A man who has never tolerated complacency and immobility for himself naturally does not accept it on the part of his drivers. But, I refuse to believe that he is a heartless monster, as some would describe him. The cynical air he likes to give himself aims more at concealing strong emotivity than anything else.'

Ferrari 312/67 F1

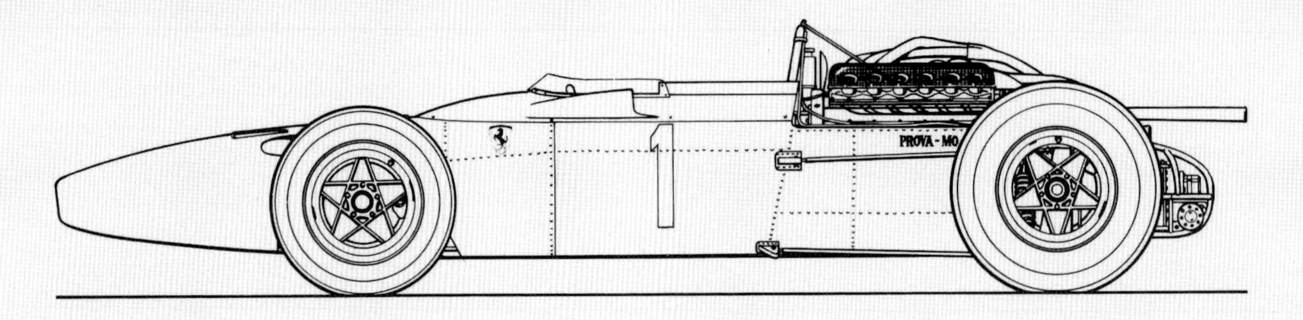

'Despite not being Ferrari's most successful entry of all time, Mauro Forghieri succeeded in designing one of the more beautiful Formula One cars of the 1960s. Perhaps overshadowed by the Scuderia's later success, Ferrari's 312 remains ... one of the most aesthetically pleasing Formula One cars of not only the 1960s, but of all time.'

– Author unknown, www.thef1times.com, 4 April 2011

Number built: Four

Engine configuration:

Type: 242 60-degree V12

Weight: 190 kilos/418.9 lbs

Construction: Light alloy block and head

Displacement: 2989.5 cc/182.4 cu in

Bore/Stroke: 77.0 mm (3.0") / 53.5 mm (2.1")

Compression ratio: 11.8:1

Valves: Three per cylinder (later four), DOHC

Fuel feed: Lucas fuel injection

Aspiration: Naturally aspirated

Power: 390 bhp/291 kW @ 10,000 rpm

Brake horsepower per litre: 130 bhp

Chassis and drivetrain: Semi-monocoque chassis, fibreglass and aluminium body panels

Front suspension: Upper rocker arms, lower wishbones, inboard spring/damper units, anti-roll bar

Rear suspension: Upper arms, reversed lower wishbones, twin radius arms, anti-roll bar

Steering: Rack and pinion

Brakes: Girling discs all round, inboard at the back

Gearbox: Ferrari Type 606, five-speed manual

Wheels: 15 inch bolt-on Campagnolo cast magnesium-alloy five-spoke wheels with Firestone tyres, 4.25/10.20-15 front and 5.50/12.20-15 rear

Drive: Rear-wheel drive

Dimensions:

Weight: 548 kg/1208.1 lbs

Length/Width/Height: 3970 mm (156.3")/720 mm (28.3")/885 mm (34.8")

Wheelbase/Track (fr/r): 2400 mm (94.5")/1551 mm (61.1")/1536 mm (60.5")

Power to weight ratio: 0.71 bhp/kg

'By any standard, 1967 was a pretty wretched year for Ferrari. Lorenzo Bandini succumbed to the terrible injuries he sustained during the Monaco Grand Prix, Günter Klass was killed instantly when his lightweight Dino slammed into a tree at Mugello and Mike Parkes broke his legs so badly in the Belgian Grand Prix at Spa that his career at the highest level was effectively finished. Ludovico Scarfiotti retired temporarily to ponder the meaning of all this, leaving just Chris Amon and me to carry on at Maranello.'

– From an article entitled *A Mexican Muddle* by Jonathan Williams

'The Maranello operation had long since been elevated from a simple business enterprise into a machine of raw jingoism for the masses. To the public the success or failure of a Ferrari car was wrapped in national honour, especially if an Italian driver was at the wheel.'

– Brock Yates, *Enzo Ferrari*, 1991

It probably also had something to do with the fact that the Vatican had taken the position that motor sport was immoral and should be made illegal. As Brock Yates pointed out in his comprehensive 1991 biography *Enzo Ferrari*, the Scuderia had become 'a national institution, a quasi-official representative of Italy on the international racing circuit' and if Church opposition was not enough, the newspapers berated Ferrari if his drivers didn't win.

Despite the Italian public's preference for Italian drivers, ever since the deaths of Eugenio Castellotti in March 1957 and Luigi Musso in July of the following year, Ferrari had simply sought the best drivers available, no matter what their nationality. 1966 had been something of a stellar year for the Scuderia, however, with its 1964 World Champion John Surtees winning at Syracuse and Spa, where he also annexed pole position and drove the fastest lap before leaving the team in the middle of the season. Ludovico Scarfiotti and Mike Parkes finished first and second in the Italian Grand Prix at Monza to near-delirious public acclaim, while Lorenzo Bandini's second place at the Monaco Grand Prix was the best of his points-scoring finishes.

This then was the background to Chris Amon's first year with Ferrari, and victory with Lorenzo Bandini in the two season-opening sports car races at Daytona and Monza had earned him a place in the F1 squad at Ferrari's first Grand Prix of 1967 in Monaco on 10 May. The car he would drive was perhaps the most beautiful single-seater ever to emerge from Maranello, 312/67 V12/0003 (he would also drive the 0005 and 0007 chassis later that year).

Ferrari 330/67 P4

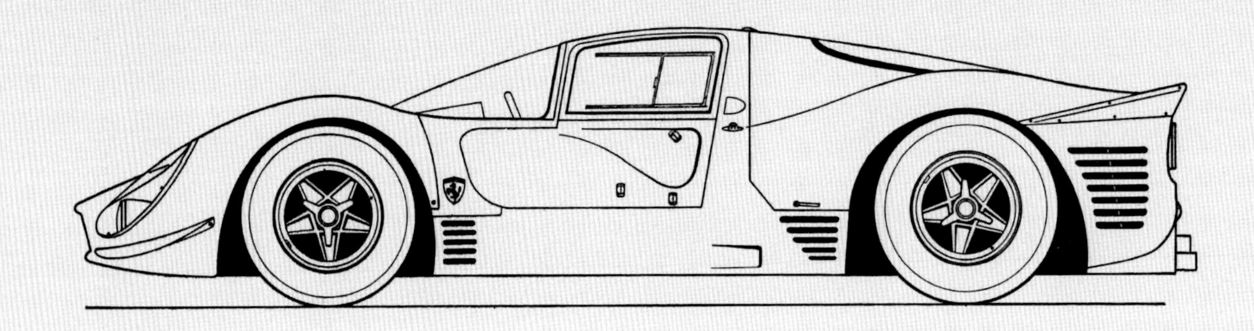

'The P4 was not only fit for purpose, inasmuch as it kept winning, it was also as voluptuous as 312/67 was svelte; it was Sophia Loren to the single-seater's Audrey Hepburn.'

Number built: Three

Engine configuration:

Type: 237 60-degree V12

Displacement: 3967 cc/242.1 cu in

Bore/Stroke: 77 mm (3.03")/71 mm (2.80")

Compression ratio: 11.0:1

Fuel feed: Lucas fuel injection

Aspiration: Naturally aspirated

Power: 450 bhp/335.6 kW @ 8000 rpm

Brake horsepower per litre: 113.44 bhp

Chassis and drivetrain: Aluminium body over tubular steel frame

Front suspension: Double wishbones with coil springs, dampers, and anti-roll bars

Rear suspension: Double wishbones with coil springs, dampers and anti-roll bars

Steering: Rack and pinion

Brakes: Ventilated discs all round

Gearbox: Ferrari five-speed manual

Drive: Rear-wheel drive

Dimensions:

Weight: 792 kg/1746 lbs

Length/Width/Height: 4216 mm (166.0")/1803 mm (71.0")/1003 mm (39.5")

Wheelbase/Track (fr/r): 2400 mm (94.5")/1488 mm (58.6")/1450 mm (57.1")

Power to weight ratio: 0.57 bhp/kg

Car 312/67 was a perfectly proportioned racing machine, uncluttered by wings and other aerodynamic devices, and it looked simply wonderful in its traditional Ferrari red livery, which bore no advertising logos beyond some discreet acknowledgements of the support of a small number of industry suppliers. The V12 engine, with its magnificent snarl of white-painted exhaust pipes, had been uprated by Franco Rocchi with reversed-flow cylinder heads. There was a new magnesium-zirconium alloy crankcase too, which would be introduced a little later, and the car would also feature a lighter five-speed transmission based on Walter Salvarani's Formula Two design. The slender Ferrari looked superb from any angle but particularly from the front. The claimed power output of 360 bhp at 10,000 rpm from the revised 36-valve engine was equally impressive, although the drivers suggested that these numbers might be somewhat optimistic.

The P4 was not only fit for purpose, inasmuch as it kept winning, it was also as voluptuous as 312/67 was svelte; it was Sophia Loren to the single-seater's Audrey Hepburn. Both were the work of that long-suffering genius Mauro Forghieri but the sports car represented the more successful blend of form and function, particularly during its first North American race at Daytona where the three Ferraris finished first, second and third, trouncing the local opposition. This was followed by victory in the Monza 1000-km event, again for Amon and Bandini, and it is fair to assume that Henry Ford II's blood pressure did

'Amon, a genial and laid-back young man with a sunny temperament but charmingly shambolic attitude towards organising his personal life, had been on the fringes of front-line Formula One since first arriving in the UK at Reg Parnell's behest in 1963. Now it seemed as though he would at last be rewarded with a car worthy of his undoubted talent.'

– From *Fifty Years of Ferrari: a Grand Prix and Sports Car racing history* by Alan Henry, 1997

NICK LOUDON

The Ferrari 330 P4 driven by Paul Hawkins and Jonathan Williams heads the winning Chaparral 2F Chevrolet of Phil Hill and Mike Spence through Bottom Bend.

not return to pre-Daytona levels until his seven-litre Mk IV won Le Mans in the hands of Messrs Gurney and Foyt, who beat Ludovico Scarfiotti and Mike Parkes into second by four laps.

In spite of his notable successes with the pulchritudinous P4, however, Chris always felt that Formula One was his focus during those days. 'Well, I enjoyed driving the sports cars, but I never got anywhere near the same satisfaction out of them and the ironical thing is that is where I was more successful but it was very much secondary in my mind.' Jonathan Williams felt the same way about sports cars too: 'I preferred open-wheelers by far. They were easier to aim and sitting in the middle is nice. Sports cars always felt sloppy by comparison.' But Enzo Ferrari, in a rare demonstration of affection for his racing cars, which he was inclined to cut up at the end of each season, apparently kept a picture of his three P4s on the last lap at Daytona for the rest of his life. After all, it really was one in the eye for his then nemesis, and Chris's former employer, the forthright Henry Ford II.

Having missed the South African Grand Prix due to sports car commitments, Ferrari's Formula One season began at Brands Hatch in the English county of Kent, where Lorenzo Bandini drove 0001 into second place in the Race of Champions just 0.4 seconds behind Dan Gurney's winning Eagle Gurney-Weslake V12, which incidentally was rated as the second most beautiful Formula One car of all time by those who compiled the survey ranking the 312 as first. The Race of Champions was also to have been Chris Amon's first for the team, but he was hurt in a collision with a female currency smuggler en route from London to Brands Hatch.

'Practice … wasn't until Friday morning,' Chris later told Alan Henry, 'but I thought I would pop down to Brands Hatch on the Thursday to see the cars being unloaded, just to have a look and be fitted into the car. I was driving my Sunbeam Tiger (a V8-engined Alpine) and a woman just turned sharply across my bows and I hit her straight in the side. I was terribly lucky, getting away with a badly bruised hand and ribs, because my passenger went right through the windscreen.' The other driver, according to the police, had a great deal of cash 'about her person' and was on her way to catch a ferry to France and, given the purpose of her trip, was probably in rather a nervous frame of mind. Chris was unable to complete more than a few laps of practice the next day before retiring due to his injuries, and so it was at Monaco that he made his first Grand Prix start for Ferrari.

The three-litre formula's second season was something Chris was well prepared for. Not only had he driven the Cooper T81-Maserati V12 the previous year in France, but he had also spent a considerable amount of time testing and racing powerful sports cars, including winning Le Mans for Ford with Bruce McLaren the previous year. During 1967, Grand Prix race wins were mainly divided between the V8 Cosworths and Australian Repcos. Jim Clark would win all the races for the Cosworth-engined Lotus team while the Brabham wins were shared between Jack Brabham himself and Denny Hulme. The three races won by V12-engined cars were down to Pedro Rodriguez campaigning the Cooper T81-Maserati, Dan Gurney in his beautiful Eagle Gurney-Weslake V12 and John Surtees driving the RA300 Honda. 1967 turned out to be very good for New Zealand, not least because Denny Hulme won the World Championship. This was despite Chris not winning a Formula One race for Ferrari that year, and that Bruce McLaren competed in a range of machines including one of his own 2.1-litre M4B-BRM cars as well as a works Eagle Gurney-Weslake V12 before the M5A that he raced the rest of the year was ready.

Probably the most outstanding individual achievement of the year was the creation of the Cosworth V8 by Mike Costin and Keith Duckworth in eight months from the drawing board to the racetrack. It appeared in Holland for the first time, won pole position and set the fastest lap on its way to winning the race. As Chris Amon told John Julian in June 2012, 'The DFV Cosworth came along and really changed the game, and whilst we were almost on level terms with the Repco, particularly once we had the four-valve head, we didn't get that until Monza. I always felt our chassis was a lot better than the Lotus 49 that year and later on, at Watkins Glen and in Mexico, I was able to stay with them, albeit with some difficulty.'

So good was the Lotus-Ford package along with the drivers that, as the season progressed, it became obvious that if the Lotus 49 stayed together it would always win. But the Australian Brabham-Repco proved to be a more reliable car and won as many championship races as the Lotus. The Brabham was powered by an uncomplicated engine, originally conceived for General Motors' Oldsmobile marque, and the team built a relatively simple, part stressed-skin-stiffened spaceframe chassis, with which they won not only the Drivers' title but also the Manufacturers' Championship in 1967 for the second year running.

Before the awful events of Monaco and Spa it seemed that Ferrari, with two championship races to their credit in the first year of the new formula, would do well again in 1967 but, unfortunately, that was not to be. Much progress was made, however, and by the end of the season the engine that had started life with 24 valves and then featured 36 was finally fielded with 48 valves in an effort to improve performance. On many occasions throughout the season it appeared that Chris would finish towards the very top of the field, whereas he scored no less than four third places, a fourth, a sixth, a seventh and a ninth and retired in only two events — in one of them, the United States Grand Prix he was in second place when the engine broke. He was also a race down on most of the rest of the field, having not contested the South African event, and although he drove alone for the bulk of the season, for he had no teammate after Spa until Jonathan Williams' appearance in Mexico, the overall championship result was a testament not only to his courage and commitment, but to the gradual but tangible improvements Mauro Forghieri had made to the car.

'Mauro Forghieri was (and is) a genius. A brilliant mind and a very likeable man too. I disappointed him when, in 1967, I told him that I wasn't able to translate Procol Harum's "A Whiter Shade of Pale" into Italian for him, which he had requested.'

– From an article entitled 'A Mexican Muddle' by Jonathan Williams

The performance of most of the new cars was impressive, to say the least, by comparison with the benchmarks set during 1966, although some cars, like John Surtees' first Honda V12, continued to disappoint. The World Championship itself turned into something of a cliff-hanger and the best in that respect for many years, for the final result was in doubt until the very last event. For the first time, the World Championship Series was staged as a two-part competition, the halfway mark being reached at the British Grand Prix in July. At that stage the drivers' five best scores counted, but since no driver had scored in all six races, the position at the end of the British Grand Prix was unaltered with Denny Hulme leading the table with 28 points from Jim Clark and Jack Brabham with 19 apiece and Chris Amon with 15.

During the latter half of the season, Hulme won the German Grand Prix, so starting the second part of his campaign at the head of the table, and although he would not win any more races, the consistency of his placing kept him close to the lead and within striking distance of the prize until the very end of the year. By the time the teams reached Mexico, had Brabham won and Hulme finished no higher than fifth, the Australian would have gained his fourth World Championship. As it turned out, Clark won the race in the Lotus 49, Brabham was second and the New Zealander, driving tactically, placed third. The competition itself was intriguing enough, but there were plenty of interesting sideshows during the course of 1967.

Tyre-wise, both Goodyear and Firestone were in the running all year, with Firestone winning six out of the Championship races, the remainder going to Goodyear. Firestone's commitment was to Chris's competitive advantage because he had done most of the tyre testing for the American company during the course of the last two years. The fuel giants in those days, like the tyre manufacturers, were among the biggest cash supporters of motor racing, but the Arab–Israeli War in the Middle East and the ensuing economic difficulties caused British Petroleum to pull out at the end of the year with Esso following suit shortly thereafter.

Shell and Castrol decided to stay in the game and Dunlop and Goodyear made it known that they would be supplying racing teams in 1968 as before. Keen followers of Grand Prix motor racing will know that it was not until the following year that sponsors were conspicuously acknowledged on the bodies and wings of racing cars. It was not difficult for non-racing regulars to overlook the contributions made by not only the tyre and fuel manufacturers but also those responsible for making component parts like brakes and brake linings, spark plugs and ignition. The two most successful fuel and oil companies in 1967 were

NICK LOUDON

Esso and BP, and those were the two which decided to pull out of motor racing. Girling and Ferodo, who made brakes and brake linings and enjoyed a virtual monopoly, won all the races between them and were good examples of companies who made the most of their motor racing investment to build their brands (Ferodo, in particular, appeared to have strategically positioned trackside advertising at almost every circuit) and to improve the quality and efficiency of their products.

The same thing went for the spark plug manufacturers and a new face in the form of NGK won its first championship motor race with John Surtees' three-litre Honda, nicknamed the Hondola, which triumphed at Monza, having been effectively rebuilt on a Lola jig and modified to UK-based Honda Racing's requirements after a less than fully competitive year, although Surtees had finished third in South Africa and would score points in three other Grands Prix during the season.

In summary, it was reckoned to be a good year for Grand Prix racing with championship wins being shared among five different marques and six different drivers, although this did not include Ferrari or Chris Amon. Some other cars appeared during the course of the season, including a couple of Formula Two Matras, but after the inconsistencies experienced during 1966, 1967 signalled the way ahead. Various ideas were discussed at length and by the end of the decade four-wheel-drive racing cars would have been tried and largely discarded, in spite of the availability of more powerful engines. As Douglas Armstrong, writing in *Automobile Year* for 1967–68, pointed out, the era of simplicity had to soon disappear in spite of the economic problems mentioned earlier if Grand Prix racing were to remain an international shop window for manufacturers' designs and innovations.

It was John Surtees' departure from Ferrari after a disagreement at Le Mans halfway through the previous season that would create the opening for Chris within the team. Surtees, the only man ever to have won World Championships on two wheels as well as four, was already much admired in Italy, having ridden for the famous Italian motorcycle manufacturer MV Agusta. He would then win the Formula One World Championship for Ferrari in the penultimate 1500 cc season of 1964 and would stay on for 1965 and the beginning of 1966, before a disagreement with Eugenio Dragoni at Le Mans outlined below. Surtees remains a very popular figure in Italy to this day.

But Ferrari was fighting on many fronts during 1965 and having declined an offer from the Ford Motor Company to buy both his road car concern and the racing team, Enzo Ferrari had incurred the wrath of Henry Ford II, who was thereafter determined to beat him at any cost. By 1965, however, a joint venture had been established with the Fiat conglomerate to make a two-litre V6 engine for production cars, a version of which would later be used in Formula Two single-seater competition by Ferrari. Fiat would manufacture

TUMBLR.COM

ABOVE
John Surtees

OPPOSITE
Mike Parkes on his way to winning the BRDC International Trophy at Silverstone on 29 April 1967.

THE CAHIER ARCHIVE

Mike Parkes at Zandvoort; he would finish fifth in his last, full Grand Prix.

both a coupé and an open two-seater, or Spyder, to accommodate this motor and the front-engined cars, known as Fiat Dinos, were to be sold without the Ferrari name, although the engine would be billed as a Ferrari design. The project was principally Fiat's with Ferrari himself advocating the engine be a three-litre flat 12 of the type that was being developed for Formula One competition, but this would have been too expensive to manufacture. The fact that Fiat's plans, rather than Ferrari's, were implemented was proof that the Agnelli family and their company were about to exert even more influence upon Ferrari, which would ultimately lead to a complete takeover.

1965 had been unsuccessful for Ferrari in Grand Prix motor racing while Jim Clark dominated the Formula One Championship with six wins in his Climax-engined Lotus 33 and would clinch the title by the middle of the season. Surtees suffered a series of mechanical failures and was handicapped by relatively low power output for the entire year. He also had problems with the team manager, Eugenio Dragoni (a friend of Enzo Ferrari with connections to the Agnelli family, who owned a cosmetics and perfume manufacturing company in Milan) who had joined the team as Mauro Forghieri took up a more senior position.

Dragoni openly favoured Lorenzo Bandini and things were made more difficult because John Surtees didn't get on very well with Mike Parkes, who tended to overlook the former's engineering skills. Parkes' father had been Chairman of Alvis, Coventry-based builders of aero engines, cars and military vehicles, and Mike had worked as an engineer with the Rootes Group so he was sometimes inclined to discount Surtees' input. As usual, Ferrari did nothing to bring peace to the proceedings for, as Brock Yates pointed out in his magisterial biography *Enzo Ferrari* in 1991, discord to Ferrari's mind was the mother of fast cars!

However, this was clearly not the case in reality because Surtees was the most talented driver on the team and in spite of Dragoni's efforts to get Bandini the best car and Parkes' run of good form, Surtees was the only man capable of keeping up with the opposition from Lotus, Brabham and BRM. He did achieve a third place at the British Grand Prix, but the season ended poorly for Ferrari's top driver in late September with a terrible crash at Mosport Park outside Toronto in Canada. Surtees was at the wheel of his own Can-Am car, a Lola-Chevrolet rather than a Ferrari, and he had been racing independently in Can-Am competition ever since Ferrari chose not to field an entry in the newly popular and increasingly lucrative North American series. The accident left him lying seriously injured in a Toronto hospital, and although his relationship with Enzo Ferrari was still close it probably spelt the beginning of the end of their alliance in the longer term.

The end, when it came, was sudden and after so much counterproductive politicking, someone was bound to lose their temper. As it turned out, it was John Surtees who did so. He had won a brilliant race on the fast Spa circuit in the rain where no fewer than seven cars crashed on the opening lap. This famous racing scene was filmed and used in John Frankenheimer's *Grand Prix* movie of that year. Eugenio Dragoni sought to criticise Surtees for not leading the entire race distance against what he described as meagre opposition and this unsurprisingly had the effect of deepening the rift between the two men.

A week later, at Le Mans, the new 330 P3 Ferrari sports car squad faced a large number of seven-litre Mark II Ford GTs including the one handled by eventual race winners Chris Amon and Bruce McLaren. Ferrari fielded three P3s with their fabulously curvy, Piero Drogo-built bodywork and Surtees was to be teamed with Parkes in the leading car while Bandini and Jean Guichet were in the second. The third machine was entered by Luigi Chinetti's NART operation for Richie Ginther, himself a former Ferrari Grand Prix driver, and Ricardo Rodriguez.

However, when Surtees arrived at Le Mans he was told that Ludovico Scarfiotti had been signed on as a third 'reserve' driver with himself and Michael Parkes — a not particularly subtle reminder that some at Maranello did not consider Surtees fit enough to run the entire distance with a single co-driver. Colonel Ronnie Hoare of the British Maranello Concessionaires team, which fielded three Ferraris at Le Mans in 1966, was apparently of the same opinion, having seen John Surtees during the ADAC 1000 km at the Nürburgring on 5 June and remarking that he looked very ill. Eugenio Dragoni asked Hoare what he thought of Surtees after the German race and Hoare repeated this observation. According to Colonel Hoare, 'That was the reason he decided to make the change at Le Mans, which infuriated John, and that was that.'

'Surtees' unfortunate departure resulted in a series of carefully choreographed farewell messages from what Brock Yates amusingly describes as the "finely tuned network of toadies and apologists for the Scuderia, who immediately began passing the word that Surtees had been fired for a variety of offences...". This was far from a fine farewell for a distinguished driver like John Surtees, who had given of his best at Ferrari, but it would remind his replacement of the dangers he faced — off as well as on the track.'

Surtees had demanded that Scarfiotti be removed, but both Dragoni and Ferrari flatly refused, the latter speaking on the telephone from his home in Modena. Surtees packed his bags the same afternoon and left for England. It was over and another World Champion had left the Ferrari team in anger. Needless to say he was immediately hired by the Cooper-Maserati squad, taking the place of Chris Amon who had driven for the Anglo-Italian marque at the French Grand Prix at Reims before leaving to continue his testing work and to drive the high-speed Ford GT40 camera cars for John Frankenheimer as the *Grand Prix* movie production followed the racing round Europe.

In the meantime, Surtees' unfortunate departure resulted in a series of carefully choreographed farewell messages from what Brock Yates amusingly describes as the 'finely

'He was a mixture of characters: you didn't deal with one person. He was one person when he was in Maranello; he ruled like a king and we were like puppets on a string. He didn't go to the races any longer and this was a great problem. In my time, there wasn't the television, which would have kept him fully in touch, so he got bits and pieces of news at third or fourth hand and it was a bit difficult. Then I'd go up to his house by the sea, on the Adriatic, and he would be another person altogether.'

– John Surtees to John Julian on Enzo Ferrari, January 2013

tuned network of toadies and apologists for the Scuderia, who immediately began passing the word that Surtees had been fired for a variety of offences, including his complaints to the press, insubordination and an alleged diminishment of his skills following his Mosport crash'. This was far from a fine farewell for a distinguished driver like John Surtees, who had given of his best at Ferrari, but it would remind his replacement of the dangers he faced — off as well as on the track.

Some believed that Franco Gozzi, Ferrari's personal assistant and later team manager, had been told to fire Surtees following the Belgian Grand Prix, but his victory had made that impossible. Others blamed the blow-up at Le Mans, maintaining that had led to his sacking. It is certain that Surtees jumped before he was pushed but Enzo Ferrari's ego would not tolerate the humiliation of a former World Champion walking out so the myth of Surtees' dismissal was peddled for some time. Funnily enough, and despite the internal *contratiempo* and what Yates described as the 'company-sanctioned misinformation campaign', Ferrari issued a typically glib and disingenuous tribute to Surtees expressing deep regret at the loss and wishing his former driver all the best!

By the end of 1966, Dragoni's politicking was even beginning to affect Ferrari. The team had suffered with the departure of Surtees and his replacement with Parkes, who was certainly a fine sports car driver but apparently not quite in the top single-seater league. Ludovico Scarfiotti, albeit a Grand Prix winner, was also better suited to sports cars although, as Gianni Agnelli's nephew, he was politically important to Dragoni. Only Lorenzo Bandini was first rate Formula One material and he was so conscious of being Italy's top racing driver, with all that entailed in terms of public expectation, that he was forced to perform beyond his emotional and physical capacity.

Part of the trouble was that Ferrari had manipulated the press over the years to the point where the loyalty of Italian motor sports enthusiasts was totally unquestioned. Somebody had to go, however, and it would be Eugenio Dragoni. According to Yates, his abrasive personality had caused turmoil throughout the organisation and, in November 1966, Ferrari made a move to replace him. His successor was perhaps not the most obvious candidate … Franco Lini was a journalist who had known Enzo Ferrari since he first reported on the team for *Auto Italia* in 1949 and had risen to become one of the nation's leading motoring writers. Lini was in Portugal covering the Rally Costa del Sol, when he received a telephone message at his hotel. It simply said 'Call Gozzi' and was therefore like many such messages Lini had received before. They usually involved a complaint about something he had written about Ferrari and thinking it was probably more of the same, Lini ignored it until he returned to Rome, where he received a call from Ferrari himself.

'You must come to Modena immediately; take the night train,' instructed the Commendatore. Lini did as he was bid and arrived at Ferrari's office early in the morning and once the latter had shown him in, he locked the door. Lini at first feared that Ferrari had lost his reason over the unremitting assaults of the press and was about to berate him, but the team principal walked back around his desk and sat down heavily in his chair. 'How much do you make each month?' he asked Lini, who told him. It was a good salary. 'Dragoni has gone', Ferrari continued, 'you must become the team manager.' The appointment was announced on national television: a two-year contract during the course of which Lini was expected to rebuild what appeared to be a team in chaos. Mauro Forghieri was working night and day with Franco Rocchi and his staff to improve the three-litre V12s because six major teams now opposed Ferrari, all with good engines. BRM had a new V12 on the drawing board to replace its quirky H16, and with the much-discussed Lotus 49 due to appear towards the middle of the following season with what would prove to be the game-changing Cosworth V8 behind the driver, progress had to be made and soon.

Clearly, Lini required another first-class driver. Bandini was consistently fast and Scarfiotti a good all-rounder but Parkes, while quick and technically very knowledgeable, was physically disadvantaged inasmuch as he was well over six feet tall, and required a longer chassis. Building such things involved extra cost during a period of fierce competition on the Grand Prix front and the no-expense-spared onslaught from the Ford Motor Company in the sports car arena was stretching budgets to the maximum. The Italian economy was in bad shape; the militant workforce to the north of the country was staging more strikes. Ferrari had been affected by a number of these during 1966 and more unrest was expected with the advent of 1967 and this during the oppressively hot summer months in Modena and Maranello. It was under these rather trying conditions that the search for a new driver began.

NICK LOUDON

Lorenzo Bandini approaching Druids Bend during the 1967 Race of Champions at Brands Hatch on 12 March. He would finish second on aggregate to Dan Gurney.

'[Ferrari] wanted a man like a Nuvolari or, God forbid, a Fangio who would compete with that brutal, heartless, unremitting determination to win at all costs.'
– Brock Yates, *Enzo Ferrari*, 1991

Ludovico Scarfiotti, winner of the 1966 Italian Grand Prix for Ferrari and a relative of the Agnelli family, was available as was Nino Vaccarella, a 33-year-old Sicilian law professor and multiple Targa Florio winner. So was Giancarlo Baghetti, who had triumphed first time out in a Ferrari Grand Prix car at Reims in 1961, having also won his first non-Championship Formula One race at Syracuse some weeks earlier. According to Yates, 'They were gentleman drivers, skilled in sports cars and on occasion capable of fast drives in Grand Prix machines. But Ferrari knew all too well that wealthy amateurs were a different breed, devoid of that cruel emptiness in the pit of their stomachs that drives the true professional. He wanted a man like a Nuvolari or, God forbid, a Fangio who would compete with that brutal, heartless, unremitting determination to win at all costs.'

At this point, the better and more experienced drivers in the shape of Jim Clark, Dan Gurney, Graham Hill, John Surtees, Jackie Stewart, Denny Hulme and Jack Brabham were all contracted to other teams, but Franco Lini had his eye on Chris Amon. As Yates put it, 'The son of a prosperous New Zealand sheep farmer, Amon had knocked around the European scene for four seasons, gaining a reputation of something of a party boy as well as a quick driver in outclassed machinery.'

Quick he most certainly was and professional too, with tens of thousands of useful miles' tyre and general testing to his credit, not to mention victory at Le Mans and increasingly promising performances among the established Formula One drivers. As for the 'cruel emptiness' referred to above, that probably wasn't how Chris felt on a daily basis, but the substance of his upbringing and a conventional education at what is still arguably New Zealand's best school equipped him with a generous measure of confidence and the ability to deal with everyone from Enzo Ferrari to a newly hired works mechanic with the same respect and consideration he brought to every encounter. He remains the only New Zealander in the history of the sport to have been a works Ferrari Grand Prix driver.

Chris was racing in the North American Can-Am series with a McLaren when he learned of Ferrari's interest in him. 'A slight, sleepy-eyed young man,' continued Yates, 'Chris Amon was hardly the prototype of the strutting, macho race driver but he was abundantly talented and was a desirable prospect for the depleted Maranello

'Once again, the Commendatore had bluffed a zealous youth into risking his life for the privilege of driving for the last "grand constructor" in the field. It was to be a dubious honour!'
– Brock Yates, *Enzo Ferrari*, 1991

contingent.' After flying to Modena and meeting with Ferrari Chris was hired for 1967, apparently agreeing to drive for no salary and 50 per cent of the purse.

The young man in question, however, made no secret of the fact that he wanted to drive for the Old Man at Maranello, for he was also a keen and knowledgeable student of Grand Prix motor racing history and he knew what it meant to follow in the footsteps of Farina and Fangio, Hawthorn and Collins, Behra and Brooks, Scarfiotti and Surtees. And by the time he reached 60, Enzo Ferrari was less tolerant of drivers or their managers' ideas of their value and respected those who made their own financial arrangements with him and subsequently justified their worth while driving his cars.

There may be no blueprint for the ideal Ferrari Grand Prix driver and many of the standard attributes required for selection could be found in men racing for other Formula One teams during that year. But if you could demonstrate the sheer artistry a car like 312/67 demanded of a racer while exhibiting the discipline and consistency of an effective test driver, the awareness blended with experience that enables you to know when to go for the quick lap in practice, and the courage and capability to take it to the limit when you do, you're some of the way there.

If you can look Enzo Ferrari in the eye aged 23 with a promising F1 track record and a win at Le Mans to your credit and convince him that you can perform, although he already knows that, which is why you are there, and if you could tell him later when the car wasn't working and why, although he probably didn't want to hear that bit because one of his trusties had already blamed the driver, and if you have the steely serenity required to rise above the riddles of Maranello politics and the fickle favours of the Italian media, you're even closer to the mark.

WWW.BOLDRIDE.COM

Chris Amon's victory with Bruce McLaren at Le Mans in 1966 was among the things that brought him to Enzo Ferrari's attention.

'It was a good time for Chris to have joined Ferrari, although I was slightly surprised because in a way he was Bruce's protégé. After the problems at Parnell Racing, Chris was a bit of a lost soul and Bruce picked him up and put him in the sports cars and, of course, he was fantastic in those. That automatically made him the Number Two driver for Formula One starting in 1966, but we only made it to Monaco with one car. Chris's car had to stay back in the workshop because there was no engine for it. And then the whole programme fell over and, incidentally, had we had enough engines and done the whole season, I would have been one of Chris's mechanics on that.

'Chris was therefore out on a limb so going to Ferrari was the great lifeline, but perhaps it didn't look that way at the beginning because Enzo had no money and he liked to play one driver off against the others, although he did realise Chris was pretty special. It must have been quite something for Chris to go there and do that, but it's also a mark of the respect Ferrari had for him.'

– Howden Ganley to John Julian, October 2012

If you can take a P4 sports car and win first time out for Ferrari at Daytona with Lorenzo Bandini and come back to Italy and do it again at Monza, and if you are brave enough to lead the team onward after the dreadful accidents that befell Bandini and Parkes at the Grands Prix in Monaco and at Spa, and if you still thrill to the sound of a Formula One Ferrari V12 catching then firing and bellowing furiously at those standing idly around before you take it onto the track and then to that intangible, invisible and ever-elusive edge: to the very brink of car control where only a few top drivers go … and if the apparently unsentimental Old Man still sends you birthday greetings, long after you have gone, it may be safe for you to assume that, like other great Ferrari drivers, not only were you at Maranello when he was, but a part of you never left.

On a less philosophical note, if you grew up on a farm, as Chris Amon and Jim Clark did, you probably had an advantage that today's karting five and six year olds might appreciate for, as Chris told John Julian in June 2012: 'I certainly think that helped in that I was driving the old farm utility around the paddocks aged six, which is a little bit similar to kids starting in karts at the same age and, by the time they are fifteen, they are very experienced drivers. I think driving needs to become a second nature and the more you do it, the more likely it is that it will.'

And there's another thing the best of these drivers shared in those days and it's fair to assume that the most gifted of their successors still do, although the controls on a 2013 Grand Prix car are very different to those you would find in the cockpit of a 46-year-old Ferrari. Aviators talk about capable 'stick and rudder men' and riders refer to 'good hands'. Racing sailors may remember the 'motion' of a yacht and if, for example, it was prone to 'weather helm' upwind or 'broaching' downwind and, in spite of today's omnipresent telemetry, some racing drivers still use the language and gestures of their predecessors when describing the handling of a car.

But there's something the very good ones have that there's no word for: the matchless eye–hand coordination and the super-sensitive foot and fingertip control necessary to drift a 1960s Grand Prix car on 1960s tyres through long, fast, bumpy bends with 1960s surfaces like Madgwick at Goodwood or Woodcote at Silverstone, before they installed the chicane, while maintaining situational awareness and inch-perfect attitude; or the deftness and focus, accuracy and consistency required to slide a car round the streets of a wet Monte Carlo lap after lap after lap without ever making contact with a barrier or another car; or the self-discipline required to 'squeeze the fear' as Gilles Villeneuve used to say, each time you took a really fast corner like the Masta Kink at Spa without lifting your right foot.

If you've got it, then you're a member of a very exclusive club, numbering perhaps 1 in 20 of all those who have ever competed in a Grand Prix car, but you may still not win a race or take the World Championship. By way of contrast, you can work extraordinarily hard at getting it, as another 1 in 20 may have done, and you can win races and Championships through sheer bloody-mindedness, perseverance, grit and tenacity and you will rightly be admired for it. But to witness one of those memorable exercises in car control that is clearly on a separate level, such as Gilles Villeneuve demonstrated to those watching his Ferrari 312T4 during the wet practice preceding the 1979 United States GP at Watkins Glen, is to watch an artist at work, and you don't really need to know a great deal about motorsport to appreciate that.

'I left in rather difficult circumstances ... and Chris went into a scene which was to a certain degree stable but did not include a natural leader.'

– John Surtees to John Julian, January 2013.

'And, because you are a driver, you rarely witness the terrible moments in the pits when a plume of smoke appears on the far side of the circuit and the commentator's voice crackles harshly over the Tannoy and says that Driver A has left the circuit at Corner B and that he will broadcast more information as soon as he receives it. Then flashing, worried glances are exchanged, an ambulance takes to the track and team members run the length of the pit lane and across the infield and another driver comes in and says it looks bad and a pretty young girl is taken to a quiet place at the back of the garage by some of the older drivers' wives and on, perhaps, to the hospital where she will either find her man alive or not, burned or with badly broken limbs.'

– John Julian

THE CAHIER ARCHIVE

CHAPTER

3

Monaco, Zandvoort, Spa, early summer

'The death of Lorenzo Bandini was an extremely painful reminder of auto racing's hazards and also testimony to the intense affection that people have for their heroes. Last Saturday 100,000 mourners attended Bandini's funeral in Milan, their grief the sharper because he had been the only Italian driver of the very highest rank. Even as those rites were observed, the Indianapolis 500 drivers, among whom a few, who had competed against Bandini in his final race at Monaco, began the risky business of qualifying. Each chanced the same end that was Bandini's, yet obviously none held back. This is racing's way and always has been — and will be as long as men choose to stake their lives on their skills and disciplined passions.'

– *Sports Illustrated*, 22 May 1967

Monaco

ACCOMPANIMENT: 'Voilà' by Françoise Hardy (1967)

Chris Amon had been to Monaco as a driver in 1963 and again in 1964, but on the first occasion he was obliged to surrender his car to his much older French teammate, Maurice Trintignant and, on the second, he failed to qualify the 1.5-litre Lotus 25-BRM V8 he was campaigning for Reg Parnell Racing. Nevertheless, he had already competed in 18 Grands Prix by this time, had won the Le Mans 24 Hour Race in a Ford Mk II with Bruce McLaren in 1966, and had started the 1967 season with sports car victories for Ferrari at Daytona and Monza with Lorenzo Bandini.

OPPOSITE
John Surtees (Honda) pursues Lorenzo Bandini (Ferrari) through the chicane leading onto the Quai Albert Premier. Bandini, tired and dehydrated, would misjudge this chicane later in the race and crash with fatal consequences.

'[Lorenzo Bandini] wasn't the controversial character I expected; he was absolutely charming.'

– Chris Amon to Eoin Young, *Forza Amon!*, 2003

THE CAHIER ARCHIVE

Lorenzo Bandini, Monaco, 7 May 1967, before the fateful race.

His Italian teammate had begun his Grand Prix career a little earlier in 1961 at the Belgian Grand Prix driving a Scuderia Centro Sud 1.5-litre Cooper T53-Maserati 4. By the time they motored down to Monaco together, Lorenzo Bandini had competed in 41 Grands Prix and had gained one win, one pole position and two fastest laps, as part of a total of 58 points. He had made his Grand Prix debut with Ferrari five years earlier in 1962 at Monaco and he returned as a likely winner during the early summer of 1967.

Chris spoke very little Italian at this stage and Lorenzo's English was not much more fluent, but they had become good friends during the short time they had raced together and very effective partners behind the wheel. Chris later told Eoin Young, author of *Forza Amon!*, an affectionate biography of the driver, 'I had the initial impression that he [Bandini] might be difficult, because of the incident in the 1964 Mexican Grand Prix when the English press concluded that he had rammed Graham Hill's BRM on purpose, but he wasn't the controversial character I expected; he was absolutely charming.' The ill-starred weekend got off to a poor start for Chris, and Lorenzo didn't arrive in Monaco until after 2 am with the first practice due to begin in a very few hours which, as Chris observed at the time, was hardly the ideal start to his Ferrari Formula One career.

The Monaco race was at an interesting stage of its development in the second year of the three-litre formula for some people felt that it might become a race for 'special' cars, rather than those fielded at other circuits during the remainder of the season. This was because the smaller, more nimble 2–2.5-litre cars could hold their own around this sinuous street circuit until the new three-litre cars has been more fully developed and established some reliability. It was because of this that the then mainstream entrants such as Ferrari, BRM, Brabham, Cooper and Lotus were joined by Formula Two cars from Matra and the occasional hybrid private entrant such as Bob Anderson's Brabham, with its four-cylinder, 2.7-litre Climax motor, which did not qualify. Sadly, Anderson, one of the last privateers, would die in a testing accident at Silverstone in the rain on 14 August 1967, as he prepared for his scheduled trip to the Canadian Grand Prix at Mosport Park, Ontario.

Most things in Monaco had not changed very much, however, and this included many of the safety features, which were beginning to look distinctly outdated at the start of an era that would see drivers embrace improvements such as harnesses and full-face Bell helmets. The spectators in those distant days included some of the same actors that had perennially populated the event, such as David Niven and other friends of Prince Rainier and his wife, the former Grace Kelly, as well as the most conspicuous couple of the mid-1960s in the shape of Richard Burton and Elizabeth Taylor, who were staying on a yacht moored close to the chicane. By the following year, they would have their own vessel, a delightful old motor yacht named *Kalizma* after their daughters, and Richard, having witnessed Lorenzo Bandini's fatal accident at close quarters, would later accept Louis Stanley's invitation to act as Patron of the Jim Clark Foundation, which campaigned for greater safety for the drivers.

Some of the stronger sources of influence were waning, however, and while at 1700 tons and 287 feet overall length Aristotle Onassis's yacht *Christina*, formerly a Canadian warship, was still the largest to be found in the harbour, he had recently relinquished his stake in the Société des Bains de Mer, which governed much of the principality's business affairs, and took little interest in the annual motor race, which was first staged in 1929 and won by William Grover-Williams in a Bugatti T35B. (He later served with the Special Operations Executive in France during the Second World War before being captured and executed at Sachsenhausen concentration camp.) But other attractions remained constant, from the celebrated Casino to the hedonism of the Hotel de Paris and from the relative comfort of the Hermitage to the more austere surroundings of the Metropole.

Many motor racing regulars would stay at the Balmoral, or 'Bad Morals' as it mysteriously became known to its patrons, the Bristol or the fading Hotel Mirabeau, down the hill from the Casino, past the Tip Top Bar, on the way to the old railway station. There was Rosie's 'Chatham' Bar, towards the top of the hill leading from Ste Devote to Casino Square, where the eponymous proprietress would deliver everything from a substantial early-morning breakfast to a withering late-night lecture if she felt that the standard of her guests' behaviour was slipping below that expected on her premises, as it sometimes inevitably did. And then there were the good, reliable restaurants like Le Bec Rouge at 12 ave St Charles, where they did those wonderful *beignets de moules* and the grilled *loup de mer* with fennel inside and Rampoldi, nearer the Casino at 3 ave des Spelugues, at the edge of the Casino Gardens, where you might have found Françoise Hardy and Johnny Servoz-Gavin, who would successfully qualify his F2 Matra, enjoying an early dinner with friends on the Friday night or a rather more muted gathering of Brabham or Lotus personnel on the Sunday, following the dreadful events of that afternoon.

Servoz, incidentally, was very much the man at Monte Carlo and would put the injured Jackie Stewart's Matra MS10 on the front row in 1968, leading for several laps before clipping a barrier, damaging a driveshaft and being forced to retire. Chris Amon was offered the ride before Servoz, but had to decline it because, although Ferrari didn't send any cars to Monaco in 1968, the Italian team refused to let him drive for anybody else, which was a pity for Chris as he could have won that race in the Cosworth-engined, Tyrrell-run Matra MS10. Of Ferrari's absence, Chris later said 'I suppose it had to do with Bandini's death the previous year.' Chris Amon would later come within an ace of winning for Matra as a works driver during 1971 and 1972.

Johnny Servoz-Gavin would retire abruptly from Grand Prix racing at Monte Carlo in May 1970 having failed to qualify his Tyrrell March 701,

GETTY IMAGES

Richard Burton and Elizabeth Taylor on board the Camper & Nicholsons motor yacht *Beatriz of Bolivia*.

TUMBLR.COM

TARINGA.NET

partly because of an eye injury sustained while rallying the previous winter, which made it difficult for him to place his car as accurately as before. A charming bohemian by nature, and a poster boy for the Summer of Love in 1967 with his long, blond hair and louche good looks, he shared his Paris houseboat with Brigitte Bardot and Olga Georges-Picot, to name but two French leading ladies, when he wasn't travelling around Europe in a horse-drawn gypsy caravan or sailing offshore.

While undoubtedly fast, he was careless, however, and as Nigel Roebuck famously observed, first in *Autosport* and later in *Motor Sport*: 'Who knows how good Johnny Servoz-Gavin really was, or what, had his sight not been damaged, he might have made of a Grand Prix career? Probably not too much, because he simply didn't *want* it enough — it got in the way of the good life. Just on the evidence of that wet morning in Casino Square, though, it seemed to me he had talent to throw away. Which, of course, is precisely what he did with it.'

Servoz might not have had a yacht in the harbour in 1967 but plenty of older and more influential people did, and there is always speculation at Monaco as to who is lunching or dining with whom on board what vessel and why. Wasn't Jean-Luc Lagardère having a party on that pretty old three-masted schooner moored close to the yacht club on Saturday night? The head of Matra, whose corporate interests ranged from telecommunications to transport systems and from missiles to motor cars, was taking a gradual but highly effective approach to racing and would win the drivers' World Championship with Ken Tyrrell and Jackie Stewart in 1969. Any knowledgeable observer, such as a journalist watching the proceedings from the quay, might have wondered what some of the guests had in common. Wasn't that group of senior executives from Ford and weren't the others members of the Agnelli and Pigozzi dynasties, the latter being the founding family of the Simca car concern?

The presence of a couple of off-duty Ferrari drivers with their girlfriends, several well-known actors and actresses, and a sprinkling of Italian and English nobility on the long, open deck of the vessel could have gone some way to disguise the possibility that the future of the sport and perhaps the motor industries was being reshaped in some way. Shaking his head at the way these things work, the man on the quay might wander back to his hotel for dinner before retiring to his room and spending an hour or so at his typewriter. It was clear that the older Ferrari driver's engineering and evaluation skills were valued as much as his race and test-driving capabilities, but would he hang up his hat for one of the top jobs at Maranello? As for Matra and Ford; well, they had already forged a partnership with the former using the latter's 1600-cc FVA Formula Two motor, but what of Simca? And weren't the Agnellis, who owned Fiat, related to the Pigozzis in some way? It was difficult enough reporting on the racing, quite apart from speculating as to who might be in control of it. Tired and now somewhat confused, the man climbed into bed and switched off the light.

By midnight on Sunday, and on happier race days than this, the winning driver and his girl could be found at the Tip Top, having attended the post-race prize-giving, along with many fellow competitors, team members, racing journalists and others there to see the fun. The Formula One family has always had a rich reservoir of highly developed humour and it was not unusual to see a group of (mostly) English pranksters, often under the supervision of Bob Dance of Lotus or Tony Cleverley of the Rob Walker team, lifting small French cars onto chairs (one for each wheel) out on the street and awaiting the return and reaction of their astonished owners before gesturing vaguely toward groups of United States Navy sailors on shore leave and moving quietly back into the Tip Top to slake their thirst. There was a small gendarmerie a couple of doors away up the hill in those days but those inside rarely ventured out to upset the *entente cordiale*!

The creativity and timing of the mechanics when it came to practical jokes was only matched by the versatility and stamina they displayed rebuilding cars overnight in smoky, poorly lit garages at circuits from Monte Carlo to Mosport, hundreds and sometimes thousands of miles from home, after practice accidents or replacing blown engines after missed gear changes or component failures rendered them useless. As Dan Gurney recalled when talking to John Julian in August 2012, 'The unsung heroes were the mechanics, they were multi-tasking supermen who did not have the substantial pyramid of a workforce behind them as it is the case in Formula 1 today.

'They were not only chief mechanics with one helper maybe, but they fulfilled the roles of engineers, data gatherers, fabricators, logistics managers and drivers of transporters. They got paid very little, often not more than £15 a week. I remember when I was with Ferrari in '59, I saw the same faces that I had seen in Fangio's day, same hard-working Italian guys. Two examples of mechanic supermen come to mind: an Australian named Tim Wall and a New Zealander called Roy Billington. Tim, who left Brabham and came with me when I started my own F1 team, lived off cigarettes and tea; Roy was Jack's chief mechanic and another marvel. The amount of things they could accomplish without sleeping was absolutely astonishing!'

In fact Monaco was already a textbook example of how difficult a modern Grand Prix mechanic's life

OPPOSITE FAR LEFT
Princess Grace and Prince Rainier.

OPPOSITE LEFT
A joyless victory for Denny Hulme at Monaco, 7 May 1967.

'The unsung heroes were the mechanics, they were multi-tasking supermen who did not have the substantial pyramid of a workforce behind them as it is the case in Formula 1 today.

'They were not only chief mechanics with one helper maybe, but they fulfilled the roles of engineers, data gatherers, fabricators, logistics managers and drivers of transporters...'

– Dan Gurney to John Julian, August 2012

could be with temporary pit facilities, no paddock to speak of, and an assortment of garages within the Principality providing makeshift accommodation for the racing cars. The Auto Palace, for example, as used for some years by BRM, consisted of one relatively large workshop with a gallery running round it and a wheezy old elevator to move the single-seaters up and down. One of the few perks enjoyed by senior mechanics, such as Roy and Tim, or Cyril Atkins and Alan Challis at BRM, was the run down to the harbour in the Grand Prix cars first thing in the morning. The rich, throaty song of the racing engines echoed through the streets of the seaside Principality as the Monegasques set out for the *boulangerie* or returned from the *charcuterie* with supplies for the day ahead, and the remaining fishermen cleared the port and headed out to work beyond the breakwater as the first of the visiting yachts began to come in.

Some small adjustments had been made to the course since the 1966 race with the start/finish line moved towards the St Dévote corner to allow a longer sprint for the line after the Gasworks hairpin. Jack Brabham started from pole position with a time of 1 minute 27.6 seconds. Next fastest was Lorenzo Bandini, alongside him on the front row, seven-tenths of a second slower. This was a good opportunity for Bandini to demonstrate that he had emerged from Surtees' shadow at Ferrari, so he was keen to make an impressive start.

Louis Chiron, the Clerk of the Course, normally dropped the flag at Monaco, but he was sometimes engulfed as the racing cars roared

THE CAHIER ARCHIVE

towards St Dévote, with those at the back of the grid already motoring extremely quickly by the time they passed him still standing on the track. The 32-year-old Italian driver and the 67-year-old Monegasque official (and *ancien pilote*, or former driver) shared a joke before the start, with Bandini warning Chiron that he would run him over if he didn't get out of the way. 'Then who will be there to wave the chequered flag for you when you win?' retorted Chiron. Tragically, Bandini would never see a chequered flag again.

Chris Amon would start on the inside of the seventh row, having experienced some difficulty with throttle response in his Ferrari, but it was his teammate who outran Jack Brabham to the first corner, which was just as well since the Brabham's Repco engine blew up in a big way, the car spun and Jack was lucky not to snag several of those following him right there on the first lap. In those days, the race was run over 100 laps of the street circuit and the halfway order was Hulme (Brabham), Bandini (Ferrari), McLaren (McLaren), Amon (Ferrari) and Hill (Lotus), and this would remain unchanged for the next 20 laps until McLaren lost time in the pits with electrical problems.

By this time, and with a reduced fuel load, Bandini had established an effective rhythm and he slowly reduced the gap between himself and Hulme to seven seconds, but the latter was equal to the challenge and held his lead with the same sort of buffer for most of the middle section of the race. The deadlock between the two leading drivers continued until Bandini began to exhibit signs of extreme tiredness and lack of concentration, positioning the car inaccurately on some corners and having difficulty holding his head up as the heat of the early summer's afternoon sapped what remained of his energy and continued to dehydrate him.

On lap 82, as he took the waterfront chicane, his Ferrari struck the barrier with its right-hand wheels and Bandini immediately lost control. The car, with one wheel torn off, hit and mounted the straw bales on the outside of the corner then flipped and landed upside down in the middle of the road with the driver trapped beneath it. Almost instantaneously the Ferrari burst into flames and by

THE KLEMANTASKI COLLECTION

ABOVE
Chris Amon at the Old Station hairpin on his way down to Mirabeau Inférieur and Portier.

OPPOSITE
Mauro Forghieri holds Chris Amon in the area close to the pit wall on the start/finish straight.

the time Bandini was extricated from the wreckage he was very badly burned and had also sustained several fractures. Bandini stood little chance. Grand Prix racing cars didn't have self-sealing fuel cells or on-board fire extinguishers in 1967, nor did the drivers have particularly effective fire-resistant overalls or full-face helmets.

There are contemporary pictures of Chris driving through those flames for the last 18 laps of the race on his way to third place behind Hulme and Hill and, 46 years later, it is still almost impossible to imagine what went through the young man's mind. Talking to Eoin Young in 2003, Chris recalled the incident as follows for both he and Lorenzo were due to fly to Indianapolis for qualifying immediately after the race at Monaco.

'Because of the terrible accident I had to make the trip alone. I knew before I left Monte Carlo that his chances of survival were minimal so it was a miserable journey. Then on the Wednesday morning I turned up at the track to try my car, only to be told that Lorenzo had died of his burns. That upset me a lot, even though I suppose I had been expecting it.'

That Chris took to the track at all says much for his constitution. The car was a two-year-old BRP chassis owned by George Bryant, stepfather to Masten Gregory, who had won Le Mans in the NART Ferrari 250 LM with Jochen Rindt in 1965 and competed in 38 Grands Prix with other teams, starting with third place at Monaco in 1957.

'I went out in the car, which wasn't especially competitive, and a rear upright broke. I was running fairly quickly when this happened and the car went into a series of spins, which seemed to last forever. After 900 feet [275 m] of this, the car finally clouted the wall, and I got out without a scratch, but the thing was it lasted so long that I had time to think, time to get frightened. After the news of Bandini's death, all sorts of things were flashing through my mind while I just sat there, waiting for it to hit. The car was damaged, but repaired in time for practice, although it never felt right because a suspension pickup point inside the monocoque had also been damaged and was flexing under load. That wasn't discovered until much later so I didn't drive it in the race, which didn't bother me overly, I must admit.'

Monaco postscript

'My most vivid memories of 1967 are sad ones. In May Mike and I met up in Monte Carlo for the Grand Prix, at which Bandini had his fatal accident. Mike and I were watching the race from the terrace of a hotel above the track. As soon as Mike realised there had been an accident he rushed off to join the Ferrari team to see if he could do anything to help. I learned the horrifying details from the news that evening.'

– Annabel Parkes Campigotto to John Julian, October 2012

Jean-Pierre Sarti (Yves Montand): 'Before you leave, I want to tell you something. Not about the others, but about myself. I used to go to pieces. I'd see an accident like that and be so weak inside that I wanted to quit — stop the car and walk away. I could hardly make myself go past it. But I'm older now. When I see something really horrible, I put my foot down. Hard! Because I know that everyone else is lifting his.

Louise Frederickson (Eva Marie Saint): 'What a terrible way to win.'

Jean-Pierre Sarti (Yves Montand): 'No, there is no terrible way to win. There is only winning.'

– From John Frankenheimer's 1966 movie *Grand Prix* ... the initial quotation was attributed to the 1961 World Champion Phil Hill by Robert Daley, author of *The Cruel Sport*, 1963

'During this time your feet have been reacquainting themselves with the position of the pedals, heels braced gently against the metal stop below. Moving your right foot onto the brake, you roll the outside of your thin-soled shoe to blip the throttle as you change down a gear, dipping the clutch as you do so. The race to come is 28 laps of a 14.10-km circuit, opened in 1921 and comprised of the roads that run between Spa, Malmedy and Stavelot. Spa is a haunting place, especially in the rain, and it is easy to let the ghosts of those drivers like Chris Bristow and Alan Stacey, who died there in 1960, crowd into the cockpit with you on a damp day, but it is hard to squeeze them out again and to find the courage to tackle the daunting Masta Kink while barely feathering the throttle on a dry day with the high kerbs and the old farmhouses to either side on the way to Stavelot. You will use more than 50 gallons of high-octane petrol, stored around the cockpit within the monocoque, and you hope that nothing will pierce its duralumin skin for you fear the conflagration that would follow.'

– John Julian

Spa-Francorchamps via Zandvoort

ACCOMPANIMENT: 'A 200 à l'heure' by Francis Lai from the Claude Lelouch movie *Un Homme et une Femme* (1967)

'No doubt if I suggest that driving a car at high speed is an art, along with music, painting and literature, I should be greeted by some very cutting remarks from students of the accepted arts; but I really do consider fast driving as an art, an essentially twentieth-century art, and one demanding as much theoretical study, natural flair, learning and practice as any of the classical arts...'

– Denis Jenkinson

The big news at Zandvoort, apart from the outbreak of war between Israel and Syria, the launch of the Beatles' *Sgt Pepper's Lonely Hearts Club Band* album and the Paris premier of Louis Bunuel's movie *Belle de Jour*, with the cool and demure Catherine Deneuve in the unlikely role of a call girl, had been the arrival of Colin Chapman's new Lotus 49 fitted with the three-litre Ford-Cosworth V8 designed and built by Keith Duckworth and Mike Costin on a Ford-funded budget of £100,000. Two of these cars were on hand for Jim Clark and Graham Hill. Ferrari had a new car too and this was entered for Ludovico Scarfiotti who, with Mike Parkes, had staged a dead heat for victory in the non-championship Syracuse Grand Prix in Sicily on 21 May. BRM fielded

THE CAHIER ARCHIVE

Dan Gurney wins at Spa-Francorchamps on 18 June 1967 from Jackie Stewart (right) and Chris Amon (left).

a lighter and slimmer P83 and Anglo-American Racers a new Eagle, which was lighter due to the increased use of titanium and magnesium. Otherwise, and not surprisingly, more drivers were seen wearing the latest fire-resistant overalls because Lorenzo Bandini's agonising last days and his subsequent demise were very much at the forefront of most of their minds.

Zandvoort is a curious place and not universally popular. The 4.3-km circuit was built using communications roads originally made by the occupying German army to a plan drawn up by the 1927 Le Mans winner S.C.H. Davis during July 1946. For the drivers it offers drifting sand, which is not good for grip and gets in the throttle slides with occasionally hair-raising results, as John Surtees would discover when his Honda's throttle jammed on Sunday afternoon. You can see most of the track from the main grandstand just on the landward side of the dunes, but the North Sea beach is not all that appealing at the beginning of June even if you do have time for a swim. Most people stay at the Bouwes, which manages to look about as forbidding as a modern seaside hotel could; a mini-golf course is one of the few splashes of colour in the immediate neighbourhood. Most people leave soon after the race on Sunday night with Schiphol airport and the Hook of Holland ferry docks conveniently situated nearby.

Chris Amon was unusually worried the night before that first Sunday in June, but his concerns had nothing to do with how best to get out of Zandvoort the following evening. He just couldn't find the reason for the excessive tyre wear he was experiencing; it wasn't the car, the tyres or the track so he thought it must be him, but as he was probably the most experienced tyre tester anywhere for big single-seaters and sports cars, that was unlikely. Furthermore, as nobody had noticed him doing anything wrong, even unsolicited suggestions were few and far between. It was most unsatisfactory!

However, there was a race to be run at 2.30 pm on that still, sunless day and Graham Hill had put his Lotus on pole position with Dan Gurney's Eagle Gurney-Weslake V12 alongside him to the left. Chris was fractionally faster than Mike Parkes with both Ferraris occupying the

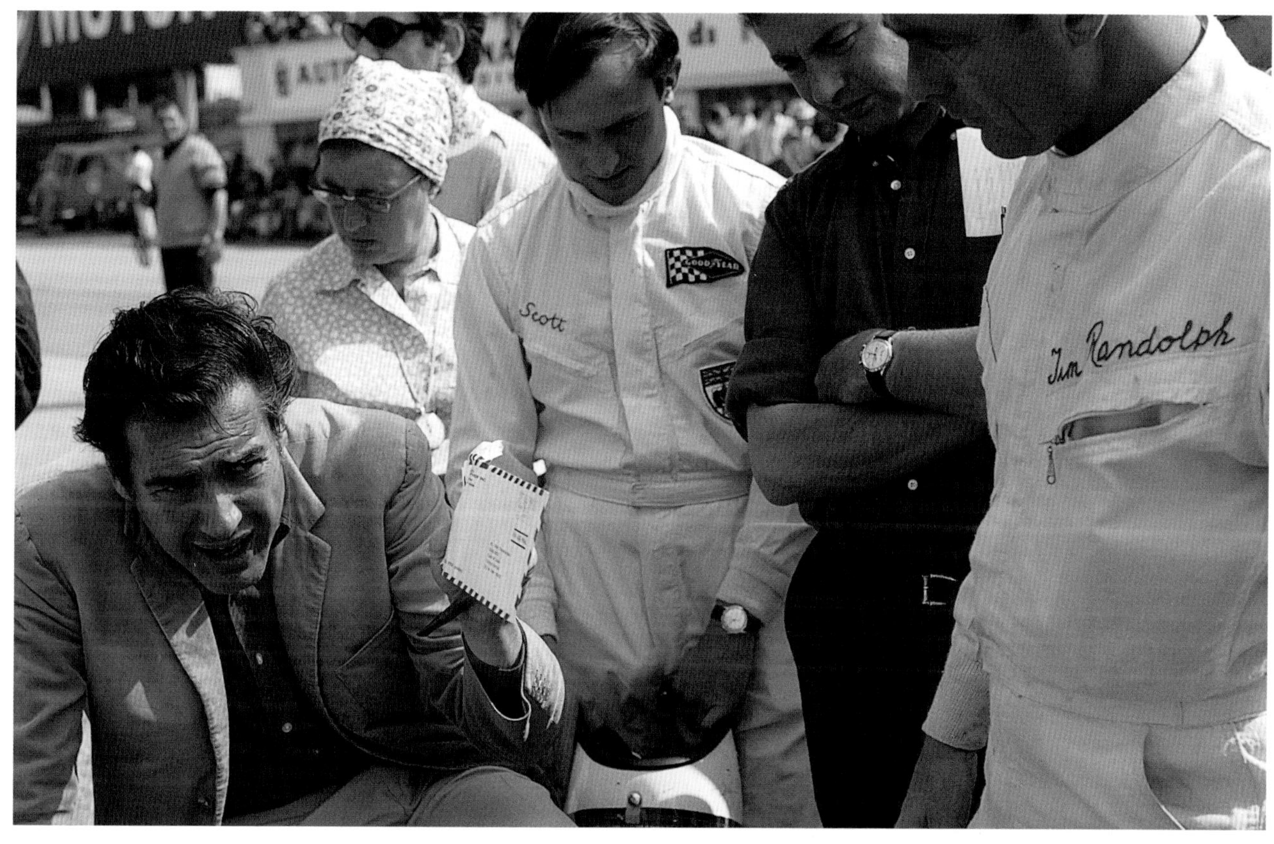

ABOVE
John Frankenheimer directs Chris Amon (in Scott Stoddard's overalls) and Phil Hill (playing Tim Randolph) in *Grand Prix*, the 1966 Metro-Goldwyn-Mayer movie epic.
The Cahier Archive

TOP RIGHT
The Oscar-winning actress Eva Marie Saint as Louise Frederickson in *Grand Prix*.
www.avsforum.com

FAR RIGHT
A *Grand Prix* movie poster featuring the cast, including James Garner playing Pete Aron and Yves Montand as Jean-Pierre Sarti.
www.avsforum.com

RIGHT
Françoise Hardy playing Lisa in *Grand Prix*.
www.avsforum.com

ABOVE

The distinctive nose of a 1967 Eagle Gurney-Weslake V12.

www.peterwindsor.com

CENTRE

Denny Hulme (foreground) and Chris Amon about to rejoin the circuit at Monza, September 1967.

Grand Prix Photo

FAR RIGHT

The artistry and intricacy of two Ferrari exhaust systems.

www.wikipedia.com (top) and The Cahier Archive

2

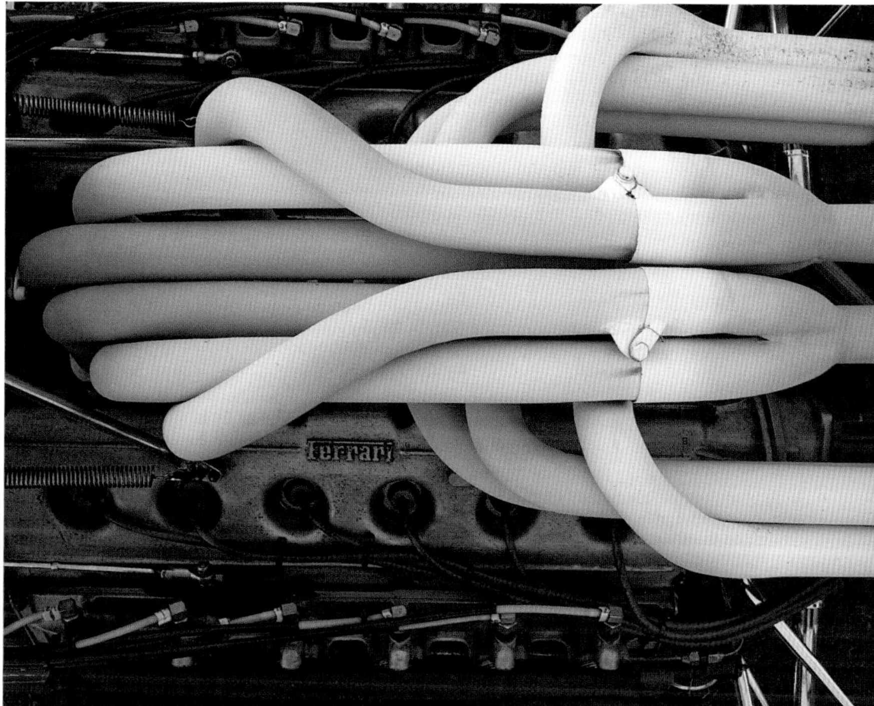
Ferrari

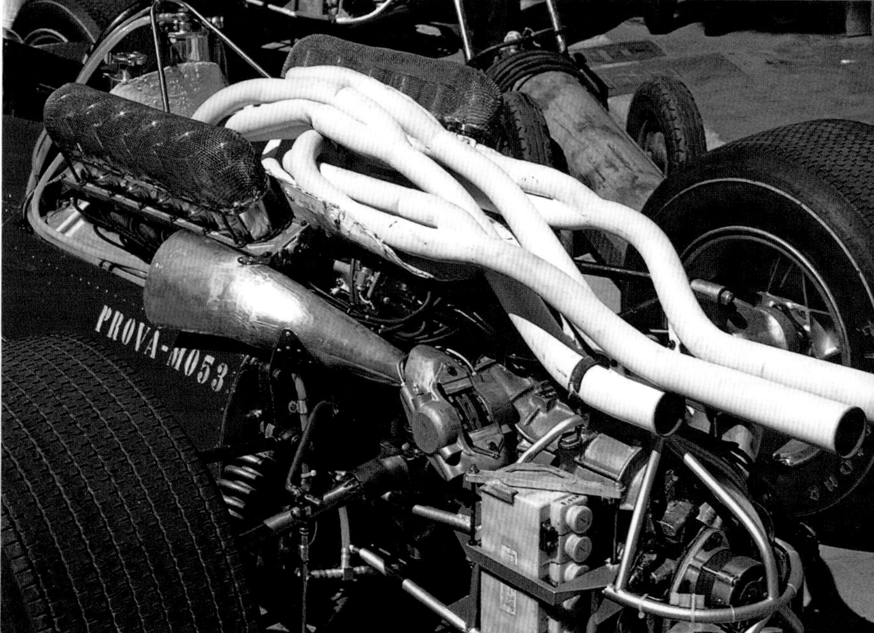
PROVA-MO53

BELOW

Graham Hill and Dan Gurney, teammates at BRM during 1960, chatting in the pits during the 1967 Monaco Grand Prix weekend.

The Cahier Archive

RIGHT

Jack Brabham, Denny Hulme, Chris Irwin, Ludovico Scarfiotti and Bruce McLaren in the pit lane at Monza.

The Cahier Archive

Johnny Servoz-Gavin took the place of an injured Jackie Stewart at Monaco in May 1968 and put his Matra MS10-Cosworth V8 on the front row, next to Graham Hill. He led for three laps before breaking a driveshaft.

Tony Stott

20

BELOW

Jim Clark talks with Graham Hill at Silverstone while Damon Hill gives them the benefit of his own view from the background!

The Cahier Archive

TOP LEFT

Denny Hulme and Jim Clark in the Mexican heat. Clark won the final round of the 1967 title race on 22 October but Hulme's third place was good enough for him to take the Drivers' World Championship.

The Cahier Archive

LEFT

A superb study of Jonathan Williams in action with his Ferrari 312/67 V12 during the Mexican Grand Prix weekend of 1967.

The Cahier Archive

OPPOSITE

Chris Amon exits the old Station Hairpin at Monaco on his way down to the waterfront. He would finish third in this, his first Grand Prix for Ferrari, which was, tragically, also the last for Lorenzo Bandini.

The Cahier Archive

ABOVE

The winning Amon/Bandini Ferrari 330 P4 during the Monza 1000 km weekend of 24–25 April 1967.

The Klemantaski Collection

RIGHT

Two of the three victorious Ferrari 330 P4s after their triumphant 1-2-3 finish at Daytona during the 4–5 February round of the 1967 FIA Group Six World Championship, which Chris Amon would win later that year. The Daytona hat-trick featured first place for Amon and Bandini, second for Parkes and Scarfiotti and third for Guichet and Rodriguez.

The Klemantaski Collection

fourth row. Scarfiotti was two rows further back on the outside of Bruce McLaren, but the latter's race would not last long with an accident on lap 2. Jim Clark, after an indifferent start, won first time out in his new Lotus-Ford, followed by the two Brabham-Repcos of Brabham and Hulme, and the Ferraris of Amon, Parkes and Scarfiotti.

Two weeks later the teams would reassemble at Spa-Francorchamps in Belgium for a warm and sunny weekend's racing over 28 laps of the fast and unforgiving 14.10-km circuit; a total of 394.80 km. Those that had returned to London between races might have taken an evening off to see the movie premier of *You Only Live Twice* with Sean Connery and Akiko Wakabayashi or *The Dirty Dozen* with Lee Marvin and Ernest Borgnine. They might have had dinner at Alvaro Maccioni's new restaurant on the King's Road or at the Steering Wheel Club in Shepherd Market, at Nick's Diner on the Ifield Road or The Place Opposite (also owned by Nick Clarke). They would most probably have heard Procol Harum's 'A Whiter Shade of Pale' for the first time on 12 or 13 June had they been to the Marquee at 90 Wardour Street or listened to the BBC or one of the remaining pirate radio stations, most of which would be closed by government decree by the end of the year. This eerie melody would turn out to be one of the surviving sounds of 1967 and the so-called 'Summer of Love' along with two of the others that succeeded it on the UK charts: The Beatles' 'All You Need is Love' and Scott McKenzie's 'San Francisco'.

Back in Belgium, sports writers were anticipating keen competition at Spa and the exploits of Eddy Merckx, who would again win the Cycling World Championship that year, were put aside, albeit temporarily. In the Hotel le Val d'Amblève on the Route de Malmedy in Stavelot, someone had left a copy of the *International Herald Tribune* on the table in the lobby and the newspaper contained a somewhat speculative report to the effect that the People's Republic of China was about to announce a successful H-bomb test while, in the United States, President Lyndon Johnson was due to meet with the Soviet Premier Alexei Kosygin in Glassboro, New Jersey for a three-day Summit Conference.

For the motor racing journalists, the first priority would be to find out what was on the agenda for the Grand Prix Drivers' Association (GPDA) meeting, scheduled for Saturday evening, which was likely to be as lively as ever at Spa given that this, the fastest road circuit in the world, was very often dry and sunny in some parts and soaking wet in others, which could mean a sudden and potentially catastrophic reduction in both traction and grip. Those present were mindful of Jackie Stewart's nasty accident the previous year, when his BRM left the track after a long, high-speed spin. The 1966 race had been run in the wet with John Surtees going straight into the lead from Jochen Rindt and Jackie Stewart, but as the cars went over the brow of the hill at Burnenville, it started to rain hard.

Some were caught out by the change in conditions and in a moment Jo Bonnier, Mike

'Spa, given the speed and the type of corners that it had, really allowed you to get the best out of a car and out of yourself and, if you could do those quick corners at an occasional eleven-tenths, it was so satisfying and gave you a tremendous thrill. I never really did enjoy the stop-start circuits, although I obviously had to contend with them and, if I went back today, I would miss some of the circuits we were able to drive on at that time.'

– John Surtees, 1964 World Champion (Ferrari) and winner of the 1966 Belgian Grand Prix (Ferrari) to John Julian, January 2013

Chris Amon approaches La Source at Spa-Francorchamps. His teammate Mike Parkes crashed on the first lap and Chris, having witnessed this awful accident, drove to a third place finish not knowing whether Mike had survived. He had, but he would never drive a Grand Prix car again.

Spence, Jo Siffert and Denny Hulme had all spun off the track with Bonnier's Cooper-Maserati hanging precariously over a sharp drop by the side of the road. Jochen Rindt then spun his Cooper-Maserati at the S-bend down the Masta Straight and, while he managed to regain control, Jackie Stewart, Bob Bondurant and Graham Hill, all in BRMs, lost it completely. Bondurant finished upside down in a ditch and was lucky to get away with cuts and bruises, but Jackie Stewart was trapped in his car and soused with petrol from a split fuel tank. Graham Hill could have continued, but seeing his teammate struggling to escape, he ran across the road and on to a neighbouring farm, where he borrowed a spanner and, together with Bondurant, finally succeeded in freeing the Scotsman by removing the steering wheel, with no marshal or medic in sight. Although Stewart's injuries were very painful, they were not life-threatening (a broken shoulder, a cracked rib and burning where the petrol had soaked his skin), but he was stuck and the consequences of the leaking petrol making contact with the superheated exhaust manifolds or brakes before he could be removed were obvious to anyone who had witnessed Bandini's fatal crash.

It wasn't just Spa that was a frequent topic of discussion at the GPDA; Rouen was another circuit where safety improvements were actively resisted and several suggestions had been made relating to the straight, wooded sections that encourage slipstreaming but offer inadequate protection for both spectators and drivers if a car leaves the road. The circuit owners were asked to put up Armco barriers, improve the surface of the track and remove the concrete bollards at a particular corner for, although these were protected by straw bales, they would constitute a lethal hazard if hit by a car. Monte Carlo had become an item in the wake of Lorenzo Bandini's fatal accident, for the use of straw bales had been condemned there as well.

Meanwhile, on that early summer's weekend in 1967, Jim Clark dominated practice in his new Lotus-Ford with a lap of 3 min 28.1 sec and the front row featured Dan Gurney's Eagle Gurney-Weslake V12 and Clark's Lotus teammate, Graham

THE KLEMANTASKI COLLECTION

'On June 18th Mike had his own accident at Spa. He was taken to a hospital in Liège where he remained for twelve days, initially heavily concussed. I dropped everything and rushed to Liege as soon as I could, staying there with my father until Mike was moved to England. I remember sitting watching him for hours to see if there was any sign of him coming out of the concussion. The hospital was doing scans every day to check there was no brain haemorrhage, and there was a risk that they might have to amputate his injured leg. Fortunately, in the end he made a very good recovery.'

– Annabel Parkes Campigotto to John Julian, October 2012

Hill, with Chris Amon on the inside of the second row. Clark led away virtually unchallenged because Hill was stuck on the dummy grid with a flat battery and Gurney had not yet selected first gear when the flag fell faster than he had anticipated.

Up the hill and into the woods of Burnenville, Clark's Lotus 49 remained firmly in front with Jochen Rindt, Jackie Stewart, Mike Parkes and the rest of the field (bar Hill) but, at Blanchimont, Parkes slid on some oil dropped by Stewart's H16 BRM and left the track, the Ferrari performing a hideous sequence of rolls that ejected the driver and left Chris Amon, observing from his racing car, quite convinced that his teammate could not have survived the crash that ensued. Sometime later the Ferrari team hung out 'Parkes OK' signs on the pit boards but Chris did not see them, partly due to the fact that he was chasing Pedro Rodriguez's Cooper-Maserati, which was living up to the nickname bestowed upon those cars: 'Torrey Canyon' (after the oil tanker wrecked off the Cornish coast of England on 18 March 1967) by spewing out oil at an alarming rate; however, this did not prevent Chris from finishing a most creditable third behind the winner, Dan Gurney, and the runner-up, Jackie Stewart.

Spa-Francorchamps has always been a circuit that favoured the brave, and the winner, Dan Gurney, also annexed the fastest lap at 3 min 31.9 sec or an average speed of 239.547 kph (148.847 mph). Chris later told Nigel Roebuck something of the accident that befell Mike Parkes that day: 'The BRMs always dropped oil at the beginning of a race. I was right behind Mike and had a bad moment on it too. He spun and I backed off — which was a mistake, actually, because you are better keeping your foot on it. He spun backwards across the road and hit the bank and then, instead of coming back onto the road, his car rolled along the bank. It was like a toy somersaulting over and over — just the most horrific bloody shunt you could imagine. Later they hung out a board telling me he was OK, but I didn't see it and drove the whole race assuming he was dead. It came so soon after Bandini's accident; that had a profound effect on me. It totally destroyed poor old Scarfiotti. He never raced a Formula One Ferrari after that day.'

'I guess things were happening in a bit of a blur, but it almost didn't pay to stop and think for too long in that suddenly the whole Ferrari thing was on my shoulders and I seem to recall trying to convince myself that I shouldn't be dwelling on it for too long, because it would get to me.'

– Chris Amon to John Julian, April 2012

THE KLEMANTASKI COLLECTION

Chris Amon at the apex of the hairpin at La Source, Spa-Francorchamps.

Lorenzo Bandini had died from the burns he sustained at Monaco in May and now Mike Parkes had been severely injured in June, to the point where he would never drive a Grand Prix car again. The 1967 season was off to a bad start. Jackie Stewart's experiences at Spa in 1966 had been the trigger for his subsequent safety crusade and this was backed to a certain degree by the GPDA, which had been established during 1961 as the successor to the Union des Pilotes Professionels Internationaux.

The GPDA had been founded at a meeting at the Hotel Metropole in Monte Carlo on 11 May 1961 and its objectives had been threefold. Firstly, it should serve as a unit that would give drivers a voice at meetings of the Commission Sportive Internationale (the then governing body of motor sport). Secondly, it should further the aims of motor racing by liaising with existing organisations and, thirdly, it should improve the safety of motor sport for both drivers and spectators. There were 18 drivers at that meeting and, for six years thereafter, Peter Garnier, then Sports Editor of *Autocar*, acted as Honorary Secretary and Treasurer and when he assumed the overall Editorship of his magazine, he was succeeded by Louis Stanley of BRM.

Garnier worked extremely hard but also wrote very amusingly about his role within the GPDA. 'This involves my going round to every member … and telling him the time and place of the meeting — "Jo Bonnier's bedroom, 2.30 this afternoon after practice." Or, as it was once at Spa, "In the field outside the Clubhouse at La Source. I can't get a room." We chose a likely looking hummock upon which to sit — which turned out to be an ant-heap!

'The meetings never start on time, a quorum seldom being present until minutes before the end; most trying are the hotel meetings held in hotel bedrooms, for invariably somebody falls into a deep sleep on the occupant's bed. I have never seen anything to approach the relaxed atmosphere in which these meetings are held; but the GPDA has made its mark within GP racing, notably in

'The [GPDA] meetings never start on time, a quorum seldom being present until minutes before the end; most trying are the hotel meetings held in hotel bedrooms, for invariably somebody falls into a deep sleep on the occupant's bed.'

– Peter Garnier

introducing such things as the dummy grid type of start, catch-tanks to keep oil off the circuit, and safety measures of one sort or another on almost all the circuits.'

The race organisers at Spa-Francorchamps, along with representatives of both regional and national government, would resist change until 1969, however, and if any driver spun off on a fast corner, he still faced the unattractive options of hitting a tree or plunging into a roadside abyss. Told that the race would be cancelled if it rained, the organisers decided to call it off. The race would become part of the calendar again in 1970, by which time more Armco barriers had been installed and a chicane sited at Malmedy. Chris Amon holds the lap record for the circuit in that configuration to this day.

Away from the circuit where Mike Parkes was so grievously injured and back on the shores of the Mediterranean, quite a lot of thought had been given as to how driver safety might be improved, not only at the scene of Bandini's crash but elsewhere and particularly in places where flammable straw bales were situated instead of barriers. In a fit of reforming zeal, the Automobile Club de Monaco bought (and borrowed) barriers after Bandini's accident and subsequent demise, but a GPDA inspector took a look behind a rather flimsy stretch of bamboo trackside fencing on the eve of the 1969 event only to discover a sheer drop of some 70 feet (21.3 m). This was subsequently remedied and those that race there (and at Spa) to this day should be grateful to Jackie Stewart, along with the pioneer members of the GPDA and others (including Louis Stanley), for doing so much to reduce the risk of death and injury to drivers and spectators alike during those cruel years.

Terrible as these events were, they were sometimes punctuated with moments of wry humour such as the exchange that took place between Jackie Stewart and Louis Stanley of BRM after Stewart's awful experience at Spa in 1966. Howden Ganley, who drove for BRM during 1971 and 1972, described it to John Julian as follows:

'You only addressed Mr Stanley as Mr Stanley; there was no question of calling him Louis, but Jackie had been given a bit of morphine after the crash and began to call him Lewis, which I suppose to a Scotsman was how it was.'

The famously patrician team principal, clearly offended by this glaring breach of protocol, peered down at his injured driver and said, 'If you must use my Christian name, would you please be good enough to employ the correct pronunciation!'

Joking apart, the accident changed Jackie Stewart who, in turn, changed Grand Prix motor racing and, by proxy, the sport as a whole. Regulations drawn up in the aftermath of Lorenzo Bandini's accident prescribed on-board fire extinguishers, a substantial roll-over bar and seat belts (or safety harnesses), although Jackie had started to use those in his BRM as early as the German Grand Prix of 1967. It was just a start, but it was a good one, a substantial foundation upon which to build, and while the nature of motor sport is essentially dangerous, risks can and have been reduced for drivers, marshals, officials and spectators alike and it is fair to speculate that, had this not been the case, Grand Prix racing could have gone the way of bullfighting.

THE KLEMANTASKI COLLECTION

Safety in 1967

'If you're involved with a high-risk strategy, you're obviously aware you can be severely injured or even killed, but that doesn't necessarily deter you from participating. … Although it was extremely dangerous during that period, different drivers had different approaches to it. Jackie Stewart, for example, and Ayrton Senna would investigate an accident very deeply to find out whether they could improve their chances of survival.

'I tended not to want to know; that was a shield against it getting to you, I suppose, so different people approach it in different ways. Many of our colleagues died in the 1960s and 1970s because the cars and the circuits were not very safe, you could almost call them the killing years, but you enjoyed the activity and felt fortunate that you could make a career out of something you really enjoyed doing and the pursuit of success helped push aside the accompanying risks. All I can do, looking back, is to remind myself how lucky I was to survive, particularly without any permanent injury.'

– Jackie Oliver to John Julian, June 2012

'I fool myself. The body of the car is like a suit of armour. Admittedly, it's only about one-sixteenth of an inch thick, but when I've got it on I feel that nothing can touch me. If you saw the road through the floorboards, you'd be very alarmed. But you don't. You're only frightened when you've lost control — and I mean *really* lost it.'

– Jonathan Williams to Richard Garrett in *Fast and Furious*, 1968

'Perhaps "fear" isn't quite the right word for what one feels. "Apprehension" might be better. One has to consider the possibility of an accident — to accept the fact that it *could* happen. Apprehension helps one to see the danger. It makes one able to sum up a situation and so it assists one's control of events.'

– Lorenzo Bandini to Richard Garrett, subsequently published in *Fast and Furious,* 1968

'Survival is the key word. Yes, there is an element of danger now, especially in the lower formulae, and while it's fairly rare now it used to be very common. A younger person might ask 'Why did you expose yourself to so much danger?' Because I loved to go fast, I loved to race, I thought it was great fun and it ultimately became my way of making a living and, at the time, earning slightly above average pay, but not much. I really did it because I loved it, notwithstanding the danger. Nowadays, even though the bottom level is pretty safe, the top level is very safe.'

– David Hobbs to John Julian, June 2012

'I did because it came with the territory. I felt I was born to race, I had an all-consuming passion for the game which required an enormous amount of concentration and thoughtful planning. The moment I did no longer have 100 per cent passion and commitment to pursue it, I quit.

'I was aware that things could go wrong; fear was my "friend", enabling my judgement to calibrate where the limits were.

'I was a student of accidents and the reasons why they might have occurred, be they human or technical. The one ingredient that no driver could count on was *luck*. One might joke that if Chris Amon did not have bad luck, he did not have any luck at all when it came to race victories. But, then again, he came out of those days alive, so in another way luck was with him too.'

– Dan Gurney to John Julian, August 2012

'We encountered it all the way up in motor racing, and in New Zealand too, so it was something that was going on all the time and, crazily, people accepted it as the norm until Jackie Stewart suddenly started telling us it wasn't, and he was right. I think for me, and for most of the others, you are so obsessed with wanting to race, to get to the top and be successful that you just put the death thing out of your mind but, in your reflective moments, you realised there was a good possibility, indeed probability, that you wouldn't survive. When I went to BRM there were three drivers, Siffert, Rodriguez and me, and at the end of the year there was only me left and I remember my mother saying to me when I went home for Christmas, "These are not very good odds, are they?"'

– Howden Ganley to John Julian, October 2012

'Let's face it; safety really came into Formula One with the money. Once Bernie Ecclestone took over the Constructors' Association, you had a more balanced situation, and you had the whole thing on television being broadcast round the world. This brought in sponsorship money, the teams began to grow, people were hired from the aerospace industries and the safety cell was developed.'

– John Surtees to John Julian, January 2013

OPPOSITE
The remains of Lorenzo Bandini's Ferrari following his accident on the eighty-second lap.

THE CAHIER ARCHIVE

'The cacophony is at its climax now with engines howling like banshees and the commentary all but obliterated. The tension in the pits and in the grandstands and on the banks and at the marshals' posts around the circuit is palpable. The drivers are looking straight down the track towards the first corner, squeezing their throttle pedals rhythmically, some with heads cocked slightly forward, all with rapidly rising heart rates, some more apprehensive than others. You touch the St Christopher medal she gave you and you reflect for a second that religion is not the only thing that sustains racing drivers at times like these. There is superstition too: you know of one driver on this grid who wears a glove inside out and another who always puts red socks on before a race.'

– John Julian

CHAPTER

4

Silverstone, midsummer, on the road with a writer

ACCOMPANIMENT: 'A Whiter Shade of Pale' by Procol Harum (1967)

'You have the dubious choice of completing your piece at the track while the traffic clears or joining the jam. You hope you will be back at your hotel in time to write your account of the weekend's activities and dictate it when the telephone call you booked earlier eventually results in a crackling connection, sometimes at a reasonable hour, say 10 pm but often much, much later. ... Perhaps someone will invent a better way of sending both words and pictures over a wire...'

– John Julian

July had been an eventful month around the world but not at Le Mans during the first weekend when a largely forgettable race had been staged at the Bugatti circuit and won by Jack Brabham from Denny Hulme and Jackie Stewart. Chris Amon was Scuderia Ferrari's only representative, with Parkes in hospital and Scarfiotti withdrawn from racing, and Amon would retire with a defective throttle cable.

Writing in *Motor Sport*, Denis Jenkinson commented as follows: 'A driving school circuit maybe (the Automobile Club de l'Ouest had laid the new track the previous year for that purpose) but not a Grand Prix circuit by European standards … yet the ACO persuaded the Automobile Club de France to hold their famous Grand Prix on the Bugatti circuit when Reims, Rouen and Clermont-Ferrand are available. Had the proposition been to hold it on the big circuit of the Sarthe, the famous 24-hour circuit, there would have been no objections but, before it took place, the famous French Grand Prix was being dubbed "The Grand Prix of the Car Parks".'

Having nothing much to report is arguably less helpful than having more than enough, particularly if you're writing for a daily newspaper or a weekly magazine and especially if you're in France. You have the dubious choice of completing your piece at the track while the traffic clears or joining the jam. You hope you will be back at your hotel in time to write your account of the weekend's activities and dictate it when the telephone call you booked earlier eventually results in a crackling connection, sometimes at a reasonable hour, say 10 pm but often much, much later. This is as tiresome for those at the receiving end in London, for example, as it is for you on the other side of the Channel. Perhaps someone will invent a better way of sending both words and pictures over a wire you hope as you wait near Reception for Madame to patch through your call. Maybe one day!

Elsewhere, a French woman named Catherine Lacoste had become the first foreigner, and the first amateur, to win the US Women's Open Golf Tournament, Nigerian forces would invade Biafra, following the latter's 30 May secession under Colonel Ojukwu and, in Britain, colour television had just started with coverage of Wimbledon on BBC2.

The race riots in Detroit, Michigan did not start until 23 July, but Motown would endure several subsequent days of unrest, looting and arson, during which 43 people were killed and 342 injured and troops patrolled the streets. It was a significant milestone on the road to the catastrophic decline of the city, its infrastructure and its great industries, among them Ford, for whom Chris and Bruce McLaren had won the Le Mans 24 Hour Race just one year earlier, but Detroit would rally for long enough to host seven Grands Prix of its own between 1982 and 1988.

Back in Britain, the Grand Prix continued to alternate between Silverstone in Northamptonshire and Brands Hatch in Kent and the two circuits could hardly have been more different; one fast, flat and largely featureless, the other with dips, swoops and cambers. In 1967 it was the turn of the former to play host to the event. Silverstone was a bomber aerodrome during the Second World War but, in August 1948, Colonel F. Stanley Barnes, Chairman of the Royal Automobile Club's Competition Committee, decided that the bleak and windy airfield behind Silverstone village was a better place for the first major motor race sanctioned by the Club, narrowly beating a similar facility named Snitterfield, near Stratford-upon-Avon, and the Grand Prix was duly held at Silverstone eight weeks later on 2 October. Two Italians, Luigi Villoresi and Alberto Ascari, finished first and second in their Maseratis and Briton Bob Gerard came third in his ERA after almost three hours and 20 minutes of racing.

Nineteen years on, the facilities at Silverstone were rather better, although many of those working there, including the staff of the British Racing Drivers' Club, were still housed in the draughty old buildings bequeathed by the Wellington bomber crews. The pits were somewhat rudimentary and the paddock something of a free-for-all, light years away from the air-conditioned trackside towers of

2013 in their secure and sanitary surroundings. As a motor racing journalist, you might have taken a stroll towards Copse Corner on the inboard side of the track that evening to the sound of The Kinks' 'Waterloo Sunset' on a nearby radio and the scent of Woodbine cigarettes behind the garages, and you would have encountered Jo Ramirez at work on Dan Gurney's Eagle Gurney-Weslake V12, which would start from the inside of the second row, and Roly Moate fettling David Hobbs's 2.1-litre BRM, entered by Bernard White, which qualified well, given its relative lack of power.

The Lotus 49s had been misfiring badly so Keith Duckworth set about the Cosworth engines the night before and traced the problem to a little bleed-hole in the fuel injection bypass system, which was admitting too much petrol, so he blocked it using a tapered pin from a sewing kit! Jim Clark had taken advantage of the absence of the forecast rain and put in a 1 min 25.3 sec with Brabham, Hulme, Gurney and Amon posting some quick laps as well. Poor Graham Hill had a nasty moment in the second Lotus 49 when, having clocked a 1 min 26.0 sec, a rear radius arm mounting gave way on the approach to the pits and the front of the Lotus was more or less destroyed when it struck the bank.

You never tire of hearing the engines either, whether en masse on the starting grid, on the overrun, or stationary in the pits. Here you may recognise the hoarse, bubbling voice of a cold Cosworth V8 being run for a few minutes after some adjustment, the impatient, sometimes fractious song of the V12 Ferrari and the unmistakable mechanical drama of the BRM H16, which is one of those multifaceted sounds that sets you listening for the smallest hint of something about to go awry.

'You never tire of hearing the engines either … you may recognise the hoarse, bubbling voice of a cold Cosworth V8 being run for a few minutes after some adjustment, the impatient, sometimes fractious song of the V12 Ferrari and the unmistakable mechanical drama of the BRM H16, which is one of those multifaceted sounds that sets you listening for the smallest hint of something about to go awry.'

Crossing the circuit to the car park, listening to the last of the commentary from the echoing loudspeakers and passing the programme sellers' canvas booths and the candy-striped tents beyond, where a limited range of refreshments is now on offer, you reflect that an entry of 21 cars and spectator numbers expected to be over 100,000 is pretty good considering the state of the British economy. There are changes being discussed, including the advent of more comprehensive television coverage, and this would no doubt help to attract other financial backers, who might not be involved with the sport in the same way as the oil, tyre and brake companies have been up until now.

There has even been talk of tobacco advertising on the cars. While this idea has not been universally endorsed, it is not without merit because the cigarette giants do have very big budgets and there's usually some PR work to be done by a competent writer. Minutes later, and oblivious to the newly posted speed limit (Transport Minister Barbara Castle has just imposed the 70 mph maximum for the UK along with the breathalyser), you are turning right into another car park. Soon you are in the friendly and familiar surroundings of the bar in the Green Man at Syresham with dinner in prospect, a bed for a couple of nights, and a relatively relaxed start in the morning before the short drive back to the track.

Bill Jupe of Ferodo has asked you to join his party tonight and Innes Ireland in his relatively new role of spectator is there and in rowdy good humour. Anthony Marsh the commentator is at the table too, along with Nick Loudon the photographer, John Glover of Champion Spark Plugs and Alan Campbell, also from Ferodo in Derbyshire. Colin Chapman looks in for a quick drink and a chat, but he has a dinner engagement elsewhere and much still to do after that. He confirms that Graham Hill will probably run tomorrow and will certainly have a car for the race, albeit 49/3, the much-modified chassis still at the works, because the front of Graham's existing car is 'a dustpan and brush job'. You will see him again the next day and hear him proclaim that 'Sixteen of us did three weeks' work overnight'. You sensibly refrain from asking him whether any of the mechanics were paid overtime for you already know the answer to that!

COURTESY OF PETERWINDSOR.COM

Both Anthony and Nick are particularly pleased to hear that Graham will be running because, as first President of the Springfield Boys Club in the East End of London, he will carry the hopes of all the youthful members, whether they be at home in Hackney or part of the group travelling to Silverstone. Anthony has worked tirelessly to promote the Club to his professional associates, many of whom have contributed both time and money to the cause, and Nick will return to London in time to drive a party of the Springfield youngsters back to Silverstone to watch the race. Anthony's gently persuasive manner has generated massive support for Motor Racing's Club for Young People, and Nick is one of many who assist the institution in any way they can.

The dinner is of the prawn cocktail and Steak *au Poivre* or melon and Chicken Maryland variety, the wine indifferent but plentiful, and the talk is of road, rather than racing cars. Colin Chapman's visit prompts some discussion of his new fibreglass-bodied, Renault-engined Lotus Europa, a small, sleek car that is definitely not for anyone over 30, nor for the claustrophobically inclined. The Ford-powered racing version is already being successfully campaigned by John Miles and Jackie Oliver. Innes has just driven the Aston Martin DBS, still with the six-cylinder Vantage motor, which he says has more room in the back for his dogs than the DB6 it replaced. He regrets selling his estate-bodied DB5, though, one of a small number he commissioned from Panelcraft in Battersea.

Bill saw Chris Amon on his way out of London in that big, handsome Ferrari 365 GT 2 + 2 coupe he keeps there, and advised that the 4.4-litre, 320-bhp V12 engine sounded as though it could do with a good run as they both turned left onto the A5 near Harpenden. Innes, who has raced Ferraris ranging from a works Formula One entry at Silverstone in 1962 to a variety of sports cars including the 250 GTO, the 275 LM, the 330P GT and the Testa Rossa, says he couldn't be doing with all those carburettors on a daily basis without a riding mechanic. A fine Grand Touring car it might be, he added, but there wasn't much point driving the Ferrari in town when no more than nine of its cylinders were working at any one time!

Bill had been in London to meet with the Banqueting Manager at the Dorchester Hotel on Park Lane and plan the annual end-of-season presentation of the Ferodo Trophy, a major motor sports award once unkindly described by a well-known motoring journalist as looking like an ice pick driven through an ashtray! He had stayed at the Washington Hotel on Curzon Street as usual and dined at the Steering Wheel Club across the road in Shepherd Market. Chris had flown with Alitalia from Milan to London and had spent a quiet night with friends at their mews house in Chelsea, having retrieved his Ferrari from a garage near Heathrow.

They ventured out for a pleasant dinner at L'Aiglon, on Old Church Street off the King's Road, and turned in well before Annabel's in Berkeley Square or any of the Chelsea nightclubs had opened. Meanwhile, back at the Green Man 48 hours on, the evening was drawing to a close. After much discussion and dissent about cars they had owned or had wanted to, all agreed that the one they would most like to try was the new rotary-engined NSU Ro 80. Nobody knew who to get hold of to arrange a test drive, although all promised to find out the next day, and so a happy, noisy dinner party reached its smoky, thirsty, sometimes raucous, albeit relatively early, conclusion.

It's half past seven in the morning and the breakfast room is already filling up fast so you wolf down eggs and bacon, Sunblest toast and home-made marmalade with Britvic orange juice and Cona coffee. By eight o'clock you are turning right onto the Dadford Road from the A43, the growling Fiat Dino barely warm, and then you turn left towards the circuit, show your press pass to the gate marshal and cross the track to the British Racing Drivers' Club and Guild of Motoring Writers' car park and switch off before lighting a Disque Bleu cigarette from a duty-free pack and pausing to plan your morning. You will later learn that the race day crowd was around 120,000

AKELTA.WORDPRESS.COM

ABOVE
Two World Champions at Silverstone: Graham Hill (1962 and 1968) and Damon Hill (1996).

OPPOSITE
Jim Clark at Becketts Corner, Silverstone with the Lotus 49, 15 July 1967.

strong. For now, you look around the car park as you make notes and see other Italian marques among the DB6 Aston Martins, 3.8-litre Jaguars and Jensen Interceptors … there is one of those handsome 2.6-litre Alfas, several Ferraris and even a left-hand-drive Lamborghini out for the day.

You write for a monthly magazine so while the copy deadline is not always so pressing you try to incorporate a bit more of the social side of racing as well and you carry a Contax camera. Today you are looking to interview one of the drivers and you would like it to be Chris Amon of Ferrari, not least because a photograph of him alongside the yellow, Bertone-bodied, Ferrari-engined Dino would please the Fiat concessionaire who has lent it to you for a long-term road test. There are no Italian drivers racing because of the loss of poor Bandini and the temporary retirement of Scarfiotti, who will return in an Eagle Gurney-Weslake V12 at Monza in early September along with Giancarlo Baghetti in a Lotus.

'… this young New Zealander alone now carries the combined hopes of Ferrari, the most famous marque in Grand Prix racing, and all who work at Maranello along with those of the many millions of Italians and others for whom Ferrari is as important as the previous year's World Cup-winning squad is to British soccer fans.'

You pause at the BRDC for another cup of coffee and a talk with the President, Gerald Lascelles, who wants to know about the little yellow coupé he saw you driving into the car park while he was finishing his breakfast in the farmhouse the Club maintains on the inside of the straight between Abbey Curve and Woodcote Corner. Next you make your way onward past a spectating Stirling Moss, who is joking with a smiling Denis Jenkinson of *Motor Sport* outside the press room (they would be demonstrating their Mille Miglia-winning Mercedes 300 SLR later in the day). And then you see Chris Amon looking at the notice board outside the Clerk of the Course's office. He turns to talk with Jim Clark and you wait for a moment before attracting his attention, mindful of the fact that this young New Zealander alone now carries the combined hopes of Ferrari, the most famous marque in Grand Prix racing, and all who work at Maranello along with those of the many millions of Italians and others for whom Ferrari is as important as the previous year's World Cup-winning squad is to British soccer fans.

Chris gives you a polite and reserved smile and says to come back after the race because there's still a bit of work to do on 0003 and that it retains the 36-valve V12, not the rumoured 48-valve unit the team is hoping for to take the fight back to the Cosworth-engined Lotus 49s of Messrs Clark and Hill, but that it may be ready for Monza. As you turn away, you glimpse Juan Manuel Fangio in a tropical suit moving through the gathering crowd towards Chris; the five-time World Champion from Argentina, who won the title for Ferrari in 1956, extends a hand to his young successor from New Zealand. He is here, like Moss, Louis Chiron and 'Phi-Phi' Étancelin, Raymond Mays and 'Toulo' de Graffenried for a gathering of the Club International des Anciens Pilotes de Grand Prix and to be reunited with their racing cars.

THE CAHIER ARCHIVE

Jack Brabham, World Champion 1959,1960 and 1966.

But when you do catch up with Chris towards the end of that weekend you forget about the yellow Dino coupé because he has a wired and wide-eyed look about him and a cigarette in his hand and he's in the garage with his overalls on. You know the adrenalin is still running hard after his titanic scrap with Jack Brabham, which lasted until just four laps from the finish, when he eventually clawed his way past the veteran Australian at the end of the start/finish straight. Giulio Borsari and the other mechanics are smiling for the first time since Monaco and munching salami from the supply they keep at the back of the transporter and sharing a bottle of Lambrusco, which may have materialised from the same secret store. They are pleased with the result and as proud of Chris as they were when he finished third at Spa, having driven all that way thinking Mike Parkes was dead.

The large crowd had evidently enjoyed it too, and all had taken great pleasure from Jim Clark's fifth British Grand Prix win. After the race, the entire Lotus team joined Jimmy on a tractor and trailer and they motored slowly round the circuit on a lap of honour, the self-effacing Scotsman shyly accepting the applause of the spectators standing on top of the earth banks around the track. Naturally, nobody knew it would be his last British Grand Prix for he would die at Hockenheim in a Formula Two race on Sunday, 7 April 1968. For now, though, this affectionate farewell was simply the perfect ending to a wonderful day.

'That race [Silverstone] was one of the most enjoyable I ever had. The Lotuses were in another race, we all knew that, so the best thing to do was just forget they were there at all. I got involved in this big dice with old Jack, and I remember he was adjusting his mirrors early in the race — and one of them flew off and whistled past my head! Then he seemed to be adjusting the other one... I've never been quite sure whether he was adjusting them or trying to tear them off...

'After about 30 laps he'd lost both mirrors, and then we had a real tussle. That was a very wide car indeed, but of course afterwards he tells me he's very sorry for chopping me all over the place but his mirrors were gone and he didn't know I was there.

'I finally passed him at Woodcote with four laps to go. He went a bit wide there and I was able to get a run at him down to Copse. But he did a good job, I must say. After I got him, I closed on Denny in the other Brabham, but there just wasn't time to catch him. I finished third.

'It was a real old-fashioned dice I had with Jack, and that was why it was so enjoyable. He was throwing everything in the bloody book at me — stones, grass, dirt, everything!'

– Chris Amon to John Julian, June 2012

THE CAHIER ARCHIVE

'One of the mechanics drove the Ferrari down to the petrol pumps at the end of the concrete square that serves as the paddock, blipping the throttle to alert those walking in front of him and sitting well up in the cockpit so that he could be sure not to run over either a sharp piece of discarded metal or glass or somebody's foot. By the time he'd brought the car back and you had climbed on board there were supposedly only 20 minutes left before the start of practice. Now it looks as though there is some sort of delay, although perhaps only for a few minutes, so you stay in the car and wriggle down into the quilted PVC cockpit liner that covers the seat, which was moulded for you at the factory, and you close your eyes for a little while...'

– John Julian

CHAPTER

5

Nürburgring, Mosport, Monza, late summer, further travels with a writer

'There's nothing quite like the Nürburgring: it's much longer than any of the other circuits for a start and, although you've raced here three times before, it's possible to lose your bearings in places along its 23.5-km length. With your eyes still shut you try to visualise the grey, serpentine ribbon of track unwinding before you and the blue dome of the sky above and the green blur of trees to either side and sometimes ahead of you on the hills beyond the long straights. Some of these seem almost uniform in height and shape while other individual trees appear taller and those at the elevated parts of the circuit just have their tips visible, waving in the wind, which makes you wonder how far you would fall if your car hurtled over the outer edge of the track.

OPPOSITE
Chris Amon on his way to third place at the Nürburgring, 6 August 1967.

'There's been a lot more attention paid to safety of late but the Grand Prix Drivers' Association is still split between those who carry on because they seem to believe they will never be touched by an accident, and others who risk the opprobrium of some members of their own profession along, perhaps, with their team and the motor racing media, for taking an active approach towards the improvement of safety standards. Excitement is one thing — that's part of your unwritten contract with the public — but you don't expect to see tightrope walkers step into space without at least making a cursory inspection of the wire that will take them across the abyss.

'This sort of waiting can make you nervous and then your mouth dries up and you wish you had sucked a boiled sweet instead of smoking that last cigarette. You open your eyes and see some activity at the end of the pit lane. At the signal from your team manager, you go through the motions of starting the three-litre V12, and then he directs you towards the back of the queue of racing cars that's begun to form. The pit marshal starts to flag the cars out onto the circuit and moments later you're accelerating hard out of the pit lane. You feel the pressure in the small of your back and can hear the rising urgency in the engine's song as you rejoin the track.

'It's a bewildering blend of fast and slow, straight and bend, crown and camber along with the jumps that lift your backside out of the seat and your feet off the pedals: those long leaps that make you hang on to the steering wheel and prompt one of those fleeting, mid-air moments, when the thought flashes through your mind yet again that you should discuss the installation of a safety harness with Mauro Forghieri. You heard that Mike's legs had been bent backwards at the knees and all the flesh raked off his shins when he was flung out of his Ferrari at Spa.

'And then your stomach lurches as you reach the sickening apogee of your flight and some bile rises into your mouth and another thought comes coursing through your mind: the fear that the car may land crabwise. Then there's a bang and a harsh, grating crunch as the suspension hits the bump-stops and sparks fly off the belly of the Ferrari and the engine undertray. There's a jolt at the base of your spine and your knees start knocking against the underside of the dashboard, and you know you'll find some big bruises in the bathtub later. Flugplatz, Aremberg, Adenau, Bergwerk, then the Karussell at Kilometre 12, where the car grounds further forward on the entrance to this banked hairpin and you tuck your head down to the left looking for the apex and avoiding the rougher patches of road surface as best you can. Hohe Acht and Wippermann are yet to come and then the Brünnchen Leap and the ups and downs which take you to Schwalbenschwanz and the run down from Kilometre 17 to Kilometre 20, the long straight that continues over the brow and takes you through the new semi-chicane, past the pits and the blurred faces of your crew and the advertising hoardings and the signals on your pit board and the fleeting glimpse you get in the mirrors of the raised arms of your timekeepers and the knowledge that it's been a quick out lap and that you've only just started.

'The adrenalin is coursing now, your anticipation and reactions sharpening, along with your visual acuity, and you're in the braking area for the first right-hander of the next lap with the engine popping and crackling on the overrun and Ickx's quick Formula Two Matra keeping to the left because he's seen you. Your eyes swiftly scan your rear-view mirrors and your feet are doing that deft, downshifting, double-declutching dance as you guide the gearlever firmly down the gate before you move your right hand back onto the steering wheel, which your left hand has just started to wind into the fast-approaching bend. A wisp of smoke curls away from your right front tyre just as you ease up on the brakes and the weight comes off it as you turn. A moment later, you are correcting a power-slide with a dab of opposite lock before squeezing the throttle hard again and glancing at your gauges, having aimed the Ferrari at the braking area before the next left-hander.'

– John Julian

THE CAHIER ARCHIVE

Denny Hulme flying the Brabham BT24-Repco V8 towards his second Grand Prix win of 1967 at the Nürburgring.

COURTESY OF THE HONDA MOTOR COMPANY

John Surtees on his way to fourth place in the last race for the Honda RA273 V12.

Nürburgring

ACCOMPANIMENT: 'Verbotene Träume' by Peter Alexander (1967)

Thinking of the timeless lines of the front-engined 250F Maseratis on show at Silverstone and how they seem to belong to another era, you reflect that it is only five years since Chris was campaigning his at home in New Zealand. And it is just 10 years since Juan Manuel Fangio amazed onlookers at the Nürburgring by catching and passing Ferrari teammates Mike Hawthorn and Peter Collins after losing a minute during a pit stop. Fangio won, setting a new lap record of 9 min 17.4 sec (91.52 mph) and winning his fifth World Championship. The cars are, by and large, still pretty, notably the Eagle Gurney-Weslake V12 and Ferrari Grand Prix machines, but there is talk in the paddock of wings appearing on the single-seaters as they have on the Chaparral 2F sports cars you saw at Le Mans.

Gunning the little Dino through the outskirts of Liege, en route to the German border and the Nürburgring beyond, you reflect upon the first half of the season. Under the present scoring system, only the five best results from the first six races are counted, with the four best from the second six retained during the second half of the season. Accordingly, Denny Hulme leads the Drivers' World Championship with 28 points from his teammate Jack Brabham and Jim Clark with Chris Amon, John Surtees and Graham Hill next in line.

Chris had returned to London, where he was looking for another flat or a mews house during one of the rare summer breaks between racing or testing commitments. He didn't get three weeks off, as some other drivers did, because of the BOAC 500-mile race for sports cars at Brands Hatch on 30 July, in which he would finish second in 330P4/0860, partnered by Jackie Stewart, thereby winning the 1967 Manufacturers' World Championship for Ferrari. Chris was also thinking about buying an aeroplane, perhaps a Piper Twin Comanche, which could make quite a lot of difference to his European racing and testing schedule. It would obviously be no help, though, as he worked his way through the North American racing itinerary, which included three Can-Am rounds.

An automatic, 1275-cc Mini Cooper S was also on the shopping list to replace the older, manual version he'd bought from Tony Maggs when they were still sharing digs with Howden Ganley, Mike Hailwood, Peter Revson and the others in Surbiton. Alec Issigonis had commissioned three of these: one for Enzo Ferrari, another for Stirling Moss and a third for Lofty England of Jaguar. They were absolutely ideal for London and it was just a question of Chris trying to persuade Alec to wangle a fourth car out of the works and sell it to him!

Ferrari, meanwhile, like most other teams, had been busy, although the Scuderia tended to go home for testing. Others had been evaluating improvements at Goodwood, Silverstone, Zandvoort or the Nürburgring itself. In fact Chris would have two Ferraris to choose from: 0005, the latest and lightest car, with a new engine and gearbox and the spare 0003, unchanged from previous races with the earlier gearbox and selector rod set-up.

Pulling into Hauptstrasse in the Eifel town of Adenau, you park outside the pink hotel used by a few of the smaller teams. Zum Wilden Schwein is only 10 minutes' drive from the circuit and the food is good so you won't have to go out tonight after a long day starting with the drive from London to Dover and a less than memorable lunch on the Zeebrugge ferry. You eat some filling local fare, including some of the hotel's namesake boar pâté followed by veal cutlets with nuts; you drink a cold Hugel Gewürztraminer and you see several of the drivers in the Formula Two field, which is part of this weekend's Grand Prix, including Brian Hart (Protos-Cosworth FVA), David Hobbs (Lola-BMW Apfelbeck), Jackie Oliver (Lotus 48-Cosworth FVA) and Alan Rees (Brabham-Cosworth FVA). Later you look into the bar, but the drivers and their girls have gone to their rooms so, with a busy weekend in prospect, you go to yours as well.

One of the funny things about this life is that you wake up in all sorts of different places and it sometimes takes you a minute or so to remember where you are and what you are up to. One glance at the safety instructions behind the door and another at the wrapper you have to unpick to get at the soap in the bathroom is enough to remind you, however, that a pig-hunter's breakfast awaits you and soon you'll be off to the track. It would be churlish to refuse the local bacon, or *speck*, so

TUMBLR.COM

The start, Nürburgring 1967.

Grand Prix drivers' wives and girlfriends

'I went into motor racing knowing no one. One of the people there was Hazel Chapman. I asked her what she was doing and she said, "Timing." I asked her if I could watch and she showed me how it was done.

'It gives me something to do. I couldn't watch Graham dicing with somebody. I'm not one of those wives who hang around. I'm one of the team.'

– Bette Hill to Richard Garrett, 1967

'Naturally, I would like to get married and settle down like everybody else, but I have not felt free to do so during my years on the race track. Of course, this is purely a personal outlook, and I know many Grand Prix drivers who are happily married and whose wives willingly accept the additional risks involved in their husbands' profession. But personally I should not feel happy about asking any girl to share those risks with me.'

– Jim Clark in *Jim Clark at the Wheel*, 1964

'As long as one races, it's not fair to have dependants. Women may say that the danger of motor racing doesn't matter; but, deep down, it does. I've seen wives who, though they'd never admit it, are terribly worried.'

– Mike Parkes to Richard Garrett, 1967

'Yes, it must have been horrendous for the wives, particularly if they had children… I wasn't married in my Formula One days. The Doghouse Owners' Club started as a mutual support group in those dark times and it moved on to be a wonderful fund-raising organisation as racing became safer and many great charities benefited from this, and I know what was involved because my wife was Chairman at one point.'

– Howden Ganley to John Julian, October 2012

TUMBLR.COM

Left to right: Nina Rindt, Sally Courage, Patty McLaren, Bette Hill and Helen Stewart.

Author's note: Howden Ganley was elected Honorary Dog (the only male member of the Doghouse Owners' Club) during the course of the 50th anniversary celebrations in 2012 and was presented with a pair of specially commissioned cufflinks in recognition of the help he had given the WMRAC over many years. Howden's wife Judy is a well-known and long-standing supporter of the Doghouse Owners' Club, having variously served as Treasurer, President, and as one of the leading cabaret stars at the WMRAC's hugely successful Charity Balls!

you help yourself liberally to that and the *ruhrei*, or scrambled egg, along with some high-octane coffee and then you smuggle out a couple of slices of local bread and some sausage to make a sandwich later!

The Dino starts willingly enough on this clear August morning and you dawdle on the way to the circuit, having refused an overt challenge from the driver of a new Porsche 911S. You are aware of the glances your pretty car is attracting and you notice, in turn, the growing number of BMW 2000 TiLux saloons, along with the occasional shapely 2000 CS coupés among the Mercedes and the smaller fry, including examples of the rear-engined Volkswagen Beetle and NSU Prinz. There are quite a few motorbikes too; BMWs mostly, but with a few touring British riders astride new Norton Commandos and some older Triumph Bonnevilles. You reach the competitors' entrance and show your armband to the marshal who waves you on because he, like you, knows there will be the usual spiel about what constitutes an acceptable credential for a journalist who also takes photographs at the paddock press desk further down the lane.

And so you ease the yellow Dino past people on foot and signs reminding you that life (or just about anything) *besser geht mit Coca-Cola* or with a packet of Roth-Händle cigarettes in your pocket. You cross the track and wave to Bette Hill as you reach the car park and remind yourself to catch up with her later. She's not at every race because of the children's school commitments and you want to talk to her about the Women's Motor Racing Associates Club, also known as the Doghouse Owners' Club, and its ongoing charitable and emergency assistance work and the eagerly anticipated end-of-season ball. The WMRAC was founded just over five years earlier, on 7 February 1962, by a group of Grand Prix drivers' wives and girlfriends and Bette was a founder member of the original committee of six under the chairmanship of Sheila Van Damm.

Fed up with the Spartan nature of British circuits and the concomitant lack of protection from the British weather, the ladies, often with children in tow, had set about making themselves more comfortable as they fed and nurtured their team members, kept lap charts and cared for those in distress after an accident. They also set up the WMRAC Benevolent Fund with this contingency in mind so that they could give financial as well as moral support to those whose husbands or boyfriends had been killed or injured, or to 'anyone connected with motor racing whose circumstances had altered through accident or illness'. Fifty years later, members of the WMRAC can take immense pride in the comfort they have brought to hundreds of women and men and the millions of dollars they have raised to support this activity.

Different wives cope with this unusual life in different ways, as do the drivers, and Bette has an understanding with Graham about telephoning when he is away without her. Accordingly, he never makes regular calls home because if he missed one, it might give her unnecessary cause for concern. Later, you ask her about the time for retirement and what a relief it will be when that day dawns. But she says it's not like that … as she once told the writer Richard Garrett, 'I know Graham knows what he is doing and I know that his head is squarely on his shoulders. I don't have any fear that he is going to make mistakes. But,' she added, 'I fear for the things he fears for. You know — the unknown things. Oil and water on the track and things like that. Perhaps a headstrong driver might make an error, which would involve him.' And you reflect, as you raise your camera to frame her handsome, smiling face, that this is another thing the GPDA handles well … a quiet word from one of the older drivers to an excitable newcomer could save a lot of pain later on, and who better than Graham to tell an overconfident young buck about the facts of life in Formula One.

The Drivers' World Championship had been split into two parts for the purposes of scoring, so Denny Hulme, who topped the table with 28 points, came to the race in a confident frame of mind. Someone in the Press Room had noted that unusually no Grand Prix had been wet to date in 1967, a situation that many felt would be corrected at the Nürburgring. As it turned out, this was not to be and a crowd of no less than a quarter of a million would arrange themselves around the Eiffel mountain course to bear witness to what was always one of the most exciting races on the Formula One calendar on a warm and sunny day.

Of the eight Formula Two drivers entered, it was Jacky Ickx who was the sensation of both practice and the race. Obliged by the rules to start behind the Formula One pack, he had posted a practice time that would have put him on the front row between Hulme and Stewart. Within six laps of the start, he had hauled his Tyrrell-Matra-Cosworth up the field into fourth place. Unfortunately, the car would succumb to suspension breakage after 12 laps of intolerable punishment over the notorious, stomach-churning Nürburgring jumps and the subsequent bone-shaking landings while charging hard in fifth place.

By this time, Dan Gurney had taken the overall lead in the Eagle Gurney-Weslake V12 and was flying, setting a new lap record of 103.148 mph. At two-thirds distance he was almost three-quarters of a minute ahead of Hulme and a second World Championship win looked likely. But, with two laps to go, a universal joint gave way to the incessant caning and Hulme was through with his teammate Jack Brabham some 40 seconds behind him with Amon harrying the Australian as he had at Silverstone; this time, though, there was no way past. The victory, Hulme's second of the season, would put him squarely on course for the Drivers' World Championship.

The author and historian Pierre Berton famously referred to 1967 as 'Canada's Last Good Year' and while there may be some that disagree with that sentiment, the Canadians certainly made the most of their Centenary celebrations from coast to coast. The country felt young and hopeful, ambitious and attractive. While Quebec was overthrowing the oligarchy of Anglophone business and Francophone clergy and hoping unrealistically for independence, most of the rest of the country was uniting under its new maple leaf flag. The economy reached its post-war peak and ordinary Canadians started to enjoy a measure of prosperity and a hand up where necessary from the welfare state.

The focus of that year's celebrations was Expo 67, the hugely successful World's Fair established on a newly created island in the St Lawrence River at Montréal, which would later become the Circuit Gilles Villeneuve in perpetuity, but a range of other attractions were scheduled, including the first Canadian Grand Prix at Mosport Park in the neighbouring province of Ontario.

Mosport

ACCOMPANIMENT: 'Canadian Railroad Trilogy' by Gordon Lightfoot (1967)

It rained at Mosport for the first Formula One race to be held in Canada, quite heavily at times, and Chris Amon was among those who spun off during the course of the event because the Firestone tyres were performing poorly in the wet on that undulating track. The field was more or less the same as at the Nürburgring without the Formula Two cars, with the exception of Messrs Pease, Wietzes and Fisher, the three privateers who were occupying the last row of the starting grid, some eight seconds off the front-row pace of Jim Clark, Graham Hill and Denny Hulme over the 2.45-mile length of the circuit. Chris qualified fourth and finished sixth behind Brabham, Hulme, Gurney, Hill and Spence and flew back to Maranello to prepare for the Italian Grand Prix at Monza on 10 September.

Denny, dozing in the cabin of an eastward-bound Boeing 707 that Sunday night, might have allowed himself one of those rare moments of quiet satisfaction at the weekend result because he was still ahead in the Drivers' World Championship and Jack's win had helped consolidate the Brabham team's position in the Constructor's rankings too. Not bad for a bloke in only his second full year in Formula One, he might have reflected, and, as anybody who ever heard him chuckle would tell you, these thoughts might have prompted a sort of sibilant 'thee-hee' from the champion-to-be as he settled back in his seat and closed his eyes.

A little later that week, Chris joined Enzo Ferrari for lunch across the road from the works as he frequently did. Roger Bailey, who worked with Chris at Maranello from the end of 1967, told John Julian 45 years later that 'it was the love of women and wine that brought them together … mostly women,' but on that day, instead of discussing girls, the Old Man wanted to tell his driver a riddle. Chris had noticed that Ferrari never directly praised or criticised a driver's performance, but he was puzzled by his employer's reference to a famous, long-departed Italian nobleman during lunch.

'I feel like the Duke of Modena,' exclaimed Ferrari over tortellini and a glass of Lambrusco. As Chris told his old friend and biographer Eoin Young some time later, 'I hadn't got a bloody clue who the Duke of Modena was and I asked someone afterwards what the Old Man was talking about. It turned out that the Duke of Modena had a mercenary army that only fought battles on fine days. The duke couldn't fight in the rain. That was his form of censure!'

'There are certain things about Monza that you never get used to, particularly as a Ferrari driver, no matter how many times you may have tested or raced there. September at Monza is perhaps the largest gathering of the Italian motor racing fanatics known internationally as *tifosi*. When you are the sole driver representative of the team they have all come to see win and expect to see win, there is nowhere to take cover. It has been a harrowing year with the loss of Bandini at Monaco and the injuries sustained by Mike Parkes at Spa and the retirement (from Ferrari) of Ludovico Scarfiotti and now you are at the home of Italian motor racing, perhaps the most spiritual Grand Prix circuit anywhere in the world, and you are among those who quite literally worship Ferrari. They fans want to see you do well, to win for them, but they can be cruelly unforgiving, should you fail to do so. Needless to say, all of the above applies to the mainstream and motor racing media too!'
– John Julian

Monza

ACCOMPANIMENT: 'La Coppia più Bella del Mondo' by Adriano Celentano (1967)

'The Palace at Monza, along with the surrounding park, used to belong to the Italian Royal Family but after King Umberto I was killed in the garden by an anarchist in 1900, his relatives felt disinclined to go back. The autodrome was built in six months during 1922, and the scale of the place is indeed majestic from the size and number of the trees to the scope of the pits and paddock. By 1967 there was an excellent restaurant, a motor museum and a funfair for those seeking refreshment or a break from the motor racing.

PICASAWEB.GOOGLE.COM

Enzo Ferrari at Monza, 9 September 1967.

'The atmosphere is further enriched by the presence of Enzo Ferrari in a lightweight suit and a broad-brimmed hat, complete with those omnipresent sunglasses, at the only practice session he cares to attend, although he will not stay for the race. The presence in the paddock of the Pope of the North, as he is irreverently known by some journalists, adds a further dollop of intrigue to the steaming cauldron of gossip, hearsay and end-of-season rumour. It is also the cause of extra pre-race nerves for those on the racing team who normally report to Mr Ferrari by telephone during the course of other race weekends and whose account of a disappointing practice session or a poor race result might be slanted against the driver rather than being blamed on, say, a lack of horsepower, which is not really what the Old Man wants to hear. Pausing in the pits with a small retinue, including Franco Gozzi, Mauro Forghieri and Franco Lini, he talks at length with Chris Amon before contemplating his red racing car in silence for several minutes more and, when he has finished, he moves on, greeting old friends and some acquaintances and signing a few autographs during the rest of his pit lane procession.

'Sometimes still, as at other circuits, you can stroll around the paddock or the infield and collect your thoughts between practice sessions or before the race; you can put on a shirt and slacks instead of your overalls and wander off in search of an espresso or you can sit behind the pits and smoke a Muratti or a more pungent Nazionale cigarette, in spite of the gravity-fed fuel delivery system that runs down the corridor at the back of the building, or you can read a book in your road car or the racing car transporter, but Monza at Grand Prix time isn't really like anywhere else. You know how different it is even as you look at the pit building from the track, the rows of eager supporters seated above the individual pit boxes with those uncomfortable little chairs bolted to the wall to the right as you look towards the track, where the drivers' wives keep time while managing to look chic and composed as they work the stopwatches and write up the lap charts.

WIKIPEDIA

Brigitte Bardot.

WIKIPEDIA

VISIT-LAKE-COMO-ITALY.BLOGSPOT.COM

ABOVE
Françoise Hardy astride her four-cylinder Honda motorcycle.

ABOVE RIGHT
The Villa d'Este and Lake Como.

'Later they will change again for a reception at the Villa d'Este; young women in pretty dresses from Emilio Pucci or Paco Rabanne, Yves St Laurent or Mary Quant, fragrant with Guerlain's Chant d'Arômes or Jean Patou's Joy; some, like Sally Courage and Nina Rindt, in demand as models themselves, enjoying the cool of early evening in the former summer residence of the Cardinal of Como. The British girls have much more to choose from in London than was the case even five years before, with expensive boutiques like Annacat on the Brompton Road, more popular shops such as Barbara Hulanicki's Biba (also in Paris), whose regular clients include Julie Christie and Brigitte Bardot, Françoise Hardy and Mia Farrow. The men are less colourfully, more conservatively attired in well-cut dark suits, plain shirts and ties; some from Hermès, others from Turnbull & Asser. There isn't much from Mr Fish or Hung on You at the Villa d'Este tonight and the worst excesses of Carnaby Street have somehow missed Formula One altogether. The only apparent sign that these fit, confident, mostly young men are not Army officers or athletically inclined merchant bankers is what they wear on their wrists: Rolex Daytona, Heuer Carrera or Breitling chronographs on the left arm and medical identification bracelets on the right!

'And so the drivers and their wives, the team managers and their patrons, be they privateers or industrialists, fuel, oil, tyre or brake men, look on as the man from Moët & Chandon performs the Cascade, where champagne poured into a glass atop a pyramid of others overflows and trickles down to fill all the glasses below. It is an attractive spectacle in the sixteenth-century, lakeside surroundings of the one-time Villa del Garovo, combining tradition, design, patience, skill and a steady hand on the part of the pourer, but occasionally there is an accident when the man loses his grip and the party atmosphere is punctured in a rain of broken glass and spilled champagne, which can deaden the atmosphere as instantly as the first report of an accident on the banking at Monza used to do. Two of the older drivers' wives present may be thinking the same thing for they glance at one another as Moët's man raises the bottle towards the peak of the pyramid. It's artistic and beautiful, but always risky and very fragile and both women have seen these things go wrong before.

'It was only a relatively short while ago that these ladies were consoling Margherita Bandini, and the Grand Prix drivers' wives have special arrangements in place, already tested in a series of emergencies, for this sort of sad contingency. Bette Hill is one of those with a bag always packed so she can take the young woman home and stay with her, in turn with others, as she starts to rebuild her shattered life and prepare herself either for a funeral or the eventual return of her badly injured man.'

– John Julian

1966 had been a great year for Ferrari at Monza for Ludovico Scarfiotti had won from Mike Parkes and both had started from the front row of the grid, with Parkes in pole position. Chris had attempted to qualify an older Brabham-BRM belonging to the film company that made *Grand Prix*, but this year he would be very much in the running, starting in fourth position on the grid with a time of 1 min 29.35 sec. Ahead of him, on the front row, was the Lotus-Ford of Jim Clark, Jack Brabham's Brabham-Repco and Bruce McLaren's McLaren-BRM.

Indeed there was room for optimism too for Ferrari had produced something new for this race in the shape of a 48-valve engine giving an apparently improved output of 390 bhp at 10,800 rpm, although the same horsepower figure had been quoted for the 36-valve unit earlier in the year. It was nevertheless surprising that only Chris was entered and even more so that Scarfiotti, having left Ferrari in the wake of Parkes' accident at Spa, should reappear driving a second Eagle Gurney-Weslake V12 with Dan Gurney who was alongside Chris on the second row.

Many maintain that Ferrari's focus for much of the 1960s remained on the sports prototypes until Le Mans was out of the way each year and only then did the Old Man and his senior staff start giving some serious thought to Formula One. Chris Amon's new car was ready, but it had only been completed the weekend before Monza, so perhaps this theory contains a measure of truth. But as Richard Garrett put it in his book *Fast and Furious*, 'Would it work this time, on the home ground, where that crowd of 80,000 people was more or less solidly behind Ferrari and where the honour of Italy seemed to depend on one young New Zealander and one unproven red car?

'On the first day of practice I came upon Chris Amon behind the pits. He seemed to be stalking the car like a hunter. It looked as if he was trying to catch it unawares and, by doing so, to discover some sort of truth about it.

'Me: "Do you like it?"

'Amon (worried): "I don't know. It's not yet as fast as the old one. We've got to get one or two things sorted out."

'Me: "Do you like the circuit here at Monza?"

'Amon (still worried): "Well — I've got to like it. It's all right. It's very fast."'

Practice, while fairly uneventful on Friday, was complicated by rain on Saturday afternoon, but Sunday was warm and sunny again and a large crowd gathered to witness what turned out to be a false start. The Cooper team had changed the battery on Jochen Rindt's car and there was a misunderstanding when an official lowered a green flag on the grid. He was in fact simply signalling the cars to move forward to the dummy grid, but Jack Brabham tore off in a cloud of tyre smoke and the race was on. The poor starter was left holding the Italian flag and looking utterly bemused!

In spite of this unexpected advantage, Jack Brabham appeared in second place at the end of the first lap, having been overtaken by Dan Gurney, followed closely by Hill, Clark, McLaren, Stewart, Hulme and Amon. The first half of the Grand Prix saw a tremendous battle for fourth place between Surtees, Amon, McLaren and Rindt and this group became as much a feature of the race as the struggle for the lead between Hill's Lotus and the two Brabhams. Clark meanwhile was regaining time he had lost during a puncture-induced pitstop and, having unlapped himself, was scything through the field.

'Monza actually wasn't too bad because the paddock area as such was fenced off and although there were a lot of people in there, it wasn't generally accessible. Probably the biggest nightmare was Silverstone ... you just couldn't move in the paddock there because anybody could walk up to the door at the back of the pits whereas at Monza and the Nürburgring you'd have people scaling the wire fencing to get a better look at you.'

– Chris Amon to John Julian, June 2012

'Sitting in your car in the pits you look forward to the point where the pit lane joins the circuit, to the pale surface of the race track beyond the starting grid, made more so by the fine cement dust used to soak up the spilled oil and you take in the contrasting greens of the woods and verges of the Royal Park where it borders the track, and you look to either side and you see people in trees and perched on top of yellow Agip advertising hoardings looking back and you begin to know how men with nets and spears, swords and shields must have felt as they steeled themselves to face the foe or the animal antagonist that awaited them in the Colosseum, where coarser sawdust was used to soak up the blood.

Recognition in 1967

'There was no international television as such. I think most of the races were filmed nationally, but you certainly weren't aware of television cameras being thrust at you on a continual basis as they are now. In fact they all seem very conscious of television cameras now because they see themselves on monitors all the time.

'I don't recall it being a problem … I remember the odd weekend off; you'd go down to the Adriatic and stay in a hotel and certainly they tended to make a fuss of you but it wasn't particularly intrusive. I mean you could go to restaurants in Modena and nobody bothered you, which is amazing when you look back at it. I went to lunch in Modena with Alexander Onassis and his two bodyguards sat at the next table and you could see the bulges in their coats but still nobody bothered you. It was just so totally different and I suppose that's because television footage was relatively rare, and while people recognised the names, they didn't always recognise the faces.'

– Chris Amon to John Julian, April 2012

'Many years after I drove for Honda at Monza, I was sitting in the Renaissance Center in Detroit when they had the Grand Prix. I was there with CBS and all the drivers had gone and I was pretty much alone in this big diner having my breakfast when this Japanese gent came over and said, "You're Mr Hobbs, David Hobbs." I said, "Yes," and he said, "I am Mr Kawamoto from Honda and I have to apologise to you. You remember you drove our car at Monza and the engine broke and I was the engine mechanic so it was my fault. I apologise!"'

'Well that was in 1988, about twenty years after the race, and around three years after that I became a member of the National Honda Dealer Council of the United States and we all went to the 1991 Tokyo Motor Show, and then about twelve of us went on to Honda and there we saw Mr Kawamoto, who by now is the head man worldwide. As we walked into his office, he said, "Ah, Hobbs-san, again I apologise profusely for you having engine failure in 1968," and all the other dealers looked at me and they couldn't believe it. The big cheese leapt up from behind his desk and came round to apologise to me!'

– David Hobbs to John Julian, June 2012

'I had an exciting time with Chris Amon and the other drivers while filming *Grand Prix*, but when John Frankenheimer told me the day I arrived in Belgium that we would be dining with the drivers that night, I actually believed that the young men at that dinner table were the drivers for the cast! I can't tell you how embarrassed I was to learn that they were the Grand Prix drivers and have no idea how I covered up my faux pas!'

– Eva Marie Saint, who played Louise Frederickson in the 1966 movie, to John Julian, August 2011.

'Adjusting your rear-view mirrors; the left one with your right hand and vice versa, you become aware of other colours, Graham Hill in Firestone-white overalls with red letters like yours, the yellow T-shirts of your own Ferrari mechanics and the Shell badges that adorn your racing car. It is a bright, hot, dusty, noisy afternoon in one of the world's great autodromes and there is that air of unremitting tension and the unspoken fear of those involved that another of their number may be culled today.'

– John Julian

At half distance Clark was seventh and with 15 laps remaining he caught Rindt and moved into fourth place. Ten laps from the end, he was almost up with Surtees' Honda and by the end of that lap he was in second place. Clark was in the lead on the last lap, but the fuel pumps on his Lotus ran dry and both Surtees and Brabham shot past before they reached Lesmo. Jack Brabham snatched back the lead at the last corner but then ran wide and lost it again down the finishing straight. John Surtees held off his old Australian rival by two tenths of one second to give the new Honda victory in its first race and to bring his own total of Grand Prix wins to six. Jim Clark, leading as the trio embarked on their last lap, having started from pole position and set fastest lap, would coast across the finishing line in third place, eight long seconds adrift. Surtees, Ferrari's 1964 World Champion, was almost lost in the wildly enthusiastic crowd that invaded the track almost as soon as he had crossed the finishing line. It was some time before he made it back to the podium where he received the winner's trophy from the courageous and elegant figure of Margherita Bandini.

The crowd was ecstatic by most international standards, although probably only at 90 per cent of the fever pitch they might have attained had Chris won the race in his Ferrari. Early on, the new car had been working and Chris had been footing it with both Surtees and Brabham for second and third places, but trouble with his rear shock absorbers and poorly performing brakes led to a couple of pit stops and a seventh place finish.

'I'm very disappointed,' he tells Richard Garrett after the race. 'There's been no real chance lately. In Canada it rained, you know. And in the starting mix-up here, I over-revved it at 2000 over the top. That's why there wasn't more power. The car's basically more competitive than any of the others.'

Richard asks him whether he has changed since arriving at Ferrari and Chris smiles. 'I think I'm a little bit harder,' he replies, 'I've learned a good many things.' Richard presses him on the question of carrying the whole weight of Ferrari's Formula One interests for so much of the season and he replies: 'No — I haven't minded. In Italy, though, in this race, it was very much a strain. So many people are looking at you. If it had been anywhere else, I might not have over-revved it at the start.'

'Amon is the hell of a nice person. He's tired now, and I'm not going to worry him any more ... I drift off into the crowd. Anyway, the Italian Grand Prix, 1967 edition, is over.'

– From *Fast and Furious* by Richard Garrett, 1968

'When they ran onto the track as they always do, they picked me up and carried me down to the pits and podium. That was their Italian sentiment.'

– John Surtees, twice victorious at Monza with Ferrari (1964) and Honda (1967), to John Julian, January 2013

THE CAHIER ARCHIVE

'The motel where everyone stays is a modest, clean and comfortable place about a mile north of the circuit on the eastern side of Route 14, and it overlooks the southern arm of Lake Seneca. This is the seventh year of Grand Prix racing at Watkins Glen, although the first motor race was run round the village streets in 1948 and the track itself was opened in 1956. Following the success of a Formula Libre race held that autumn, Cameron Argetsinger, whose family remains well-known in the neighbourhood, persuaded 2500 locals to pony up the money necessary to bid for and stage a Grand Prix. This they duly did and the race, won by Innes Ireland in a Lotus, was very well attended, so the motel, which was the only one that offered a restaurant too, benefited accordingly.

'It's Saturday night and the last day of September and Chris Amon is in his room on the ground floor of the Glen Motor Inn. He's tired after practice and the cumulative effect of a lot of travel this year, and he doesn't feel like doing any more than having a light supper in the dining room and going to bed early. There's a party of people going to Pierri's in Painted Post, a popular Italian-American restaurant owned by a family of Ferrari fans, but he pleads fatigue and a busy day tomorrow and promises to see them at the circuit over the race weekend...'

– John Julian

CHAPTER

6

Watkins Glen and Mexico City, autumn

OPPOSITE
Jonathan Williams in his Ferrari 312/67 V12 at the 1967 Mexican Grand Prix.

'Chris puts on a shirt and a knitted silk tie, a jacket and slacks from Battistoni in Rome and a pair of black Gucci loafers and makes his way to the restaurant within the hotel where Keith Ballisat of Shell approached him last year and asked whether he would be interested to meet Enzo Ferrari the following week. Chris was 23 then with a Le Mans win under his belt and some promising Grand Prix performances to his credit and he brokered his own business arrangements. Twelve months on, he leads a Ferrari team, which started 1967 with four drivers in the Formula One squad, one of whom died at Monaco, the second of which was badly injured at Spa, while the third effected a temporary retirement from Formula One or, at least, from the Ferrari Grand Prix team.

'And so, aged 24 now, Chris has shouldered the responsibility of leading the Scuderia for the best part of the season and he has scored third places at Monaco, in Belgium, at Silverstone in England and at the Nürburgring in Germany in addition to scoring points in Holland and at Mosport Park in Canada. So he greets Vic Franzese, who owns the Glen Motor Inn and whose father built it in 1947.

'Vic's grandfather moved from the Abruzzo region of Italy, around Pescara, to the United States about the turn of the century so it's fair to assume there's some local support for the men from Maranello, but the proprietor entertains all the teams every year so wisely keeps his counsel. Vic takes him to a table in the corner. Chris nods to Dan Gurney, Jim Clark and Graham Hill, and then Bruce and Patty McLaren come in and he waves them over. Vic's wife Linda arrives and everyone orders dinner and chats about the following weekend's Monterey Grand Prix, which is actually the next Can-Am race at Laguna Seca.

'Unlike some drivers, Chris doesn't have any trouble sleeping the night before practice or a race, nor does he wake up with the yips. It will only be as he waits to get in the car that those feelings of apprehension try to pile in on him as he grinds out a last cigarette underfoot. But he knows that they won't be there when the starter's flag falls, particularly if it's Tex Hopkins doing the honours and he's wearing that lavender suit, which is enough to make anyone laugh. Then he'll drop the clutch and the feelings won't return until the next time.

'For now, he stays awake in his ground floor room and reads a little from the paper he found there when he returned. *The Watkins Glen and Schuyler County News* has a round-up of odd but interesting things that have happened in the United States and elsewhere during the preceding month, and there's the *Newsweek* he picked up at the airport.

'Back in Britain, an eccentric named Bates has established a Principality on board a Second World War anti-aircraft gun platform off the Essex coast, and British Rail has announced the formal end of steam traction in the north-east of England. A new liner named *Queen Elizabeth 2* has just been launched at Clydebank while, on this side of the Atlantic, an American yacht named *Intrepid* has successfully defended the America's Cup from the advances of an Australian vessel called *Dame Pattie*; the United States has performed another nuclear test in Nevada, no doubt by way of response to those carried out by the USSR in the Semipalatinsk region of the Kazakh SSR, and Gladys Knight and the Pips have just released as a single their version of 'I Heard it Through the Grapevine' on the Motown record label in Detroit.

'Meanwhile, in Washington DC, President Lyndon B. Johnson expressed his sorrow that war was still a fact of life in the twentieth century as he bestowed the Congressional Medal of Honor upon a 21-year-old sergeant in the US Army's 1st Cavalry Division for exemplary conduct during an intense firefight with North Vietnamese troops.

‘Far away in New Zealand, home to farm and family, a year that started with an explosion and 19 fatalities at the Strongman Mine near Greymouth draws to a close with an agreement to extend licensing hours in pubs and hotels around the country.

‘“And this weekend I represent New Zealand, having flown from London to drive for the Italian Ferrari team in the United States Grand Prix at a place called Watkins Glen. What a world!” thinks Chris as he turns out the light. “What a life!”’
– John Julian

Watkins Glen

ACCOMPANIMENT: ‘Music to Watch Girls By’ written by Sid Ramin and Tony Velona (1967) and sung by Andy Williams

Most would agree that Watkins Glen in October is about as pleasant a place as you could want to race as the season draws to a close. This was the seventh time the Grand Prix of the United States had been run on the 2.3-mile circuit near Syracuse in upstate New York and the weather, when it is good, is of the very best New England fall variety: crisp sunny days with azure skies and cool, clear, starlit nights, with the maple trees beginning to shed their glorious, fiery leaves. But it’s not guaranteed!

Practice had been something of a Lotus benefit and everybody was well used to that because since they had appeared at the third race of the year in Holland, Colin Chapman’s DFV-powered cars had been consistently the fastest on the track, taking pole position in all the subsequent seven races they had entered. Their reliability had been less promising, however, and neither was in contention for the Driver’s Championship at Watkins Glen: that would be between Jack Brabham and his teammate Denny Hulme. Friday’s weather had been dismal, with low cloud closing airports and local visibility ranging from 20 to 500 metres but, as the weather improved, both Clark and Hill posted faster times with Clark emerging the quicker of the two.

Saturday was a clearer day and late in the practice session Jim Clark posted 1 min 6.07 sec, breaking the 125 mph average speed mark and seemingly securing pole position. Graham Hill was determined not to be done out of the $1000 bounty (part of a generous prize pool of $142,000 for the event) so, with Clark testing his car’s handling on full tanks, Hill snatched pole position from him with a time of 1 min 5.48 sec. Dan Gurney was a popular third in his Eagle Gurney-Weslake V12 with Chris Amon fourth fastest in his new Ferrari, chassis number 0007, before the engine broke.

Sunday’s weather was of the textbook autumn type, however, and some 80,000 people made their way to the circuit. Walter Hayes, Public Affairs Director of Ford at Dagenham in England, who had sponsored the development of the Cosworth-Ford V8, arranged a coin toss between the two Lotus-Ford drivers and proposed that the winner of that should be allowed to win the race, should both cars be in contention at the end. The drivers agreed and decided that the arrangement should be reversed in Mexico.

At the start, the two Lotus cars leapt into the

lead and by the end of the first lap Hill led from Clark, Gurney, Brabham, Amon and McLaren. Chris Amon was in typically tenacious form and was closing the gap on the Lotus pair when he lost four seconds trying to lap Jo Bonnier's Cooper. He closed again, gaining ground in the sharper corners but losing on the exits to the faster ones. Graham Hill lost the lead to Jim Clark when his clutch seized and he was briefly unable to change gear. As Clark pulled ahead, Amon caught Hill on Lap 65 and as the Lotus driver struggled with his transmission, the Ferrari took second place.

Chris Amon then saw his oil pressure drop on Lap 76 whereupon Graham Hill moved ahead again but, after eight more laps spent wrestling with his gearbox, Chris overtook him again, holding second place until Lap 96 when his engine lost the last of its oil. This left Hill and Clark to dispute the race as originally anticipated by Walter Hayes. With Hill too far behind to maintain his claim on the first position he had 'won' the night before, Jim Clark seemed the most likely victor. Then, halfway through Lap 106, the top right-hand rear suspension link broke, causing the wheel to lurch inward. Graham Hill was 45 seconds behind at this point with two laps to run but only 23 seconds in arrears as the Lotus cars entered the final lap. Both ailing machines limped round for the last time with Clark crossing the line some six seconds ahead of Hill, Hulme, Siffert, Brabham and Bonnier.

'We stayed in an apartment in Mexico City; I still have no idea who arranged this. We would have splendid breakfasts in a place nearby of pancakes smothered in maple syrup [this was an Aunt Jemima's Pancake House according to Chris, more than 40 years on, and the peach pancakes with whipped cream and syrup were the ones to go for!]. There was a rental car which Chris drove, and after the race we visited the pyramids and motored down to Acapulco and stayed in a beautiful beachside hotel, the Pierre Marques. I don't know how Chris knew of this place. It was practically empty except for Rob Walker and Jo Siffert and we spent a few delightful days chatting by the pool.'

– Jonathan Williams to John Julian, June 2012

Mexico City

ACCOMPANIMENT: 'If I had a Hammer' by Trini Lopez (1963)

There are times when being a Formula One Team Manager makes life seem pretty good, albeit hectic, and there are others when you'd cheerfully volunteer to do almost anything else. The good news was the fact that 19 of the 20 invited entries for the Mexican Grand Prix were ready for the first four-hour practice session on Friday afternoon, but there was bad news inasmuch as the missing car (Jochen Rindt's Cooper) had been withdrawn due to some unpleasantness over starting money, which the team had demanded but nobody was prepared to pay.

BRM had brought the three cars fielded at Watkins Glen; two engines had been flown back to England to be rebuilt and the one in Jackie Stewart's car was changed as a precaution, but the new V12 that had just been tested at Goodwood failed to turn up.

Ferrari had brought the same two cars for Chris Amon and Jonathan Williams down from Watkins Glen and both engines had been returned to Modena for an overhaul and sent back across the Atlantic. That they had arrived was not in doubt for an exasperated Franco Lini had been trying desperately to liberate them from the Mexican Customs authorities throughout the Thursday night.

Practice began only 20 minutes late, although Fisher couldn't get going immediately because some gearbox parts had only just arrived. Solana's Lotus was found to have bearing problems so the mechanics set about replacing the Cosworth V8 as the other cars began to make their way onto the circuit. Further up the pit lane, Amon's Ferrari was ready to take to the track but Williams' sister car would require another two hours' work.

Jonathan Williams' path to the top echelon of motor sport was, like Chris Amon's, not completely conventional. Certainly, he had competed in the lower formulas, but that was in Europe, where he had done extraordinarily well driving for the de Sanctis Formula Three team. By the end of 1966 he had eight Formula Three wins to his credit and was one of the most conspicuously successful young drivers of his generation.

Accordingly, it was not so surprising that he was introduced to Enzo Ferrari by Goaccino Vari who owned the Ferrari dealership in Rome where Jonathan then lived. Together they went to Maranello one Sunday and Jonathan signed a contract. But in many ways it was not the golden opportunity he had hoped for, and by the end of 1967 he went to Mexico with some reluctance, bidden by Franco Lini, but with no promise that he might actually drive the Formula One car.

At the sharp end of the starting grid were Lotus, who had three cars for Clark, Hill and Moisés Solana, an occasional Formula One driver, who had competed in every Mexican Grand Prix from 1963, and two United States Grands Prix in '65 and '67, so his ninth fastest time was particularly creditable, although the Lotus was obviously competitive. Chris Amon was second on the grid between Jim Clark on pole and Dan Gurney. Behind these three were Hill, Brabham and Hulme, the latter two being the only men with a chance of winning the World Championship for Drivers. The day of the race was clear but promised to be very hot and this added to the mechanics' last-minute workload as they cut more

THE CAHIER ARCHIVE

Chris Amon, Mexico City: a fuel pump failure cost him second place in this final round.

'My method was always to start gently and work myself in. Here was an unknown circuit in a car I had never driven. I think that if I had had the car fitted for my physical size, and been allowed to drive in both practice sessions, I would have finished in the points.'
– Jonathan Williams

THE JONATHAN WILLIAMS COLLECTION

THE CAHIER ARCHIVE

ducts and louvres in the bodywork and enlarged the radiator openings. Brabham went even further and his mechanics were seen shaping a new water pipe, which they fitted along the outside of the cockpit less than two hours before the start.

The flag fell after a fashion at 1430 as advertised, but the starter had performed some kind of Mexican wave, which Clark didn't recognise, so he hesitated for a moment. Gurney, starting right behind him, ran into the back of the Lotus, damaging an exhaust on Clark's car and puncturing his own radiator. Skewered, Gurney could only raise his arm and watch helplessly as the cars streamed past him.

Graham Hill passed Chris Amon for the lead at the end of the straight and, as the cars completed the first lap, the order was Hill, Amon, Clark, Brabham, Solana and McLaren, with Williams lying twelfth in the second Ferrari. At the halfway stage, having taken the lead on Lap Three, Clark was 34 seconds clear of Amon and 47.5 seconds ahead of Brabham while Williams was enjoying a spirited scrap with Jean-Pierre Beltoise whose car appeared to be handling better than the Ferrari, but which was slower on the straight. Nothing much changed for another 10 laps except that two young spectators were nearly killed by Pedro Rodriguez when they decided to run across the track.

As the race entered its final stages, Jim Clark set a new lap record on Lap 52 of 1 min 48.13 sec (166.47 kph), having driven with a broken clutch since Lap 3. Hulme was lapped by Clark on Lap

62, which was when Chris Amon failed to appear. Chris's second-place Ferrari had run out of fuel at the hairpin bend and he climbed out and took off his helmet looking very unhappy. The leaders tore past and then, as the noise receded, he suddenly heard the ticking of his fuel pump slow as it scavenged more petrol. The engine cut out and restarted several times and then as he reached the finish, Clark went by to take the chequered flag. The lap charts had Amon in fifth place while Brabham appeared to be second as his was the only car to remain on the same lap as the winner. Denny Hulme was a lap down on the leader, but this was good enough for him to claim the 1967 Drivers' World Championship.

Mike Spence, Pedro Rodriguez, Jean-Pierre Beltoise and Jonathan Williams arrived at the finish close together ahead of Jo Bonnier and Guy Ligier who were four laps down. The official results took a long time to prepare because, according to the regulations, the last lap of any car must be within twice the time of the winner's fastest lap and Amon's had been more than this. After much deliberation the officials disallowed the Ferrari's last circuit, which put him three laps behind the winner, behind Williams and in front of Jo Bonnier.

OPPOSITE TOP
Jo Siffert enjoys a ride back to the pits with Jonathan Williams!

OPPOSITE LOWER
Having won first time out with the Honda RA300 V12 at Monza, John Surtees would retire at Watkins Glen and finish fourth here at Mexico City.

Footnote to Mexico City

Jim Clark had once again proved, as if it were necessary, what an outstanding driver he was. Sadly, his friends and rivals, along with his many supporters, would only see him in action in a Grand Prix car one more time, at Kyalami in South Africa, early the following year before he was killed in a Formula Two race one wet afternoon at Hockenheim. It was a crushing blow for his family and fans as well as for his team and the sport as a whole. These were dangerous times, but nobody had thought that could happen to Jim. As Chris Amon recalled while talking with John Julian nearly 45 years later, 'It was a major jolt to everybody.' Jim Clark had stayed with Chris and his parents at home in New Zealand during the 1968 Tasman Series in January. On 7 April, the greatest driver of his generation had gone.

'I remember going to Jimmy Clark's memorial service at the Scottish Church near Sloane Square in London; I was with Mike Spence and we were sitting together. Mike and I were weeping openly when we left the church because the thing about Jimmy getting killed was like Ayrton Senna's death many years later: people like Jimmy Clark just don't get killed. Two weeks later, I was at Mike Spence's funeral because he stood in for Jimmy at Indianapolis and crashed on the first day he was there. He hit the wall and the wheel came over and struck him on the head. 1968 was a particularly bad year because we lost Jimmy and Mike, Scarfiotti and Schlesser over such a short time.'

– David Hobbs to John Julian, June 2012

'If you are a car constructor and you want to be sure of victory you cannot do better than to study the Ford strategy for the Le Mans 24-hour race. You build the biggest, most rumbustious engine that the regulations allow. You sign on as many crack drivers as you can get. You invest enough money to keep the economy of some lesser South American republic happy for the next decade. And you turn up with masses of cars.'

– From *Fast and Furious* by Richard Garrett, 1968

THE KLEMANTASKI COLLECTION

CHAPTER

7

Sports cars

'The marshals could see the flames from the car which was now well alight and they came running. There were four of them and three gendarmes and they soon had the fire out and were searching frantically for the driver — me. They were looking around in the ditch wondering where I was, and I remember walking up the ditch, feeling a bit battered, and tapping a gendarme on the shoulder and saying, "Here I am." Poor guy; he bloody nearly died of fright!'

– Chris Amon

Le Mans

Having suffered something of a mauling at the hands of the Ford Motor Company, and most notably in the form of Messrs Amon and McLaren at Le Mans the previous year, Enzo Ferrari again pondered the idea of building a more powerful, six-litre prototype for the faster circuits while employing the 2.4-litre version of the Dino, developed, tested and raced by Jonathan Williams, on the slower ones. Eventually, he would produce a four-litre car, to be campaigned on all the tracks, and this exceptionally handsome P4 would take the title, or Speed and Challenge Cup as it was known in 1967, with 34 points from Porsche with 32 and Ford with 22.

While some of Ford's senior people might have given the impression that they dearly wanted to win the Unlimited Category of the Manufacturers Trophy as well as seeking victory at Le Mans, it was the latter that was of paramount importance to them and they seemed not to take the other races quite so seriously after A.J. Foyt and Dan Gurney had won it for them in their Ford Mk IV. Porsche continued to impress with increasingly efficient-looking racing cars and drivers like Vic Elford and Paul Hawkins, Jo Siffert and Bruce McLaren. Both the German and American concerns, particularly the latter, had racing budgets which were disproportionately large by comparison with that of Scuderia Ferrari.

Firestone had financed Ferrari's trip to Daytona where they spent a whole week practising, an

OPPOSITE
Chris Amon in the Ferrari 330/67 P4 he shared with Jackie Stewart for the BOAC 500 Mile race at Brands Hatch. They would finish in second place behind the Chaparral-Chevrolet of Phil Hill and Mike Spence and thereby secure the 1967 FIA Group Six World Championship.

THE KLEMANTASKI COLLECTION

THE KLEMANTASKI COLLECTION

exercise the team from Maranello had never previously been able to afford. And while Ferrari had modified the 1966 P3 quite substantially, the 1967 Fords were also much improved from the previous year, based as they were on the Le Mans winner with all the lessons learned with it. There was also a new car designated the Mark IV with a light alloy sandwich structure such as that employed in the primary wing structure of contemporary light aircraft. The cars, however, were rather overweight, due in part to Ford's insistence on making them as safe as possible, for team members were mindful of the fact that they had lost Walt Hansgen at the Le Mans practice weekend the year before, while Ken Miles, a most accomplished driver, had been killed in mysterious circumstances in the 'J' car during testing at Riverside in California. This Mark IV prototype also featured aluminium honeycomb chassis construction with a 'bread van' body and a Kamm-type tail. Aside from these three protagonists, there were a number of privateer Fords and Ferraris, as well as Porsches and an American Chaparral-Chevrolet 2F driven by Phil Hill and Mike Spence in the running, but this retired three-quarters of the way through the race with transmission failure.

Because of Lorenzo Bandini's fatal accident, Chris had a new co-driver at Le Mans. 'I was sharing an open P4 with Nino Vaccarella. I elected to use the open car because it was more comfortable — and it was fortunate I did because it was easier to get out of too.'

It was a race full of promise with an entry list to match and some seasoned commentators, including Nigel Roebuck and Jabby Crombac, thought there might never be such a gathering at Le Mans again for there were Fords for Dan Gurney/A.J. Foyt; Bruce McLaren/Mark Donohue; Mario Andretti/Lucien Bianchi; Denny Hulme/Lloyd Ruby; Paul Hawkins/Ronnie Bucknum and Frank Gardner/Roger McCluskey. Furthermore, there were works P4 Ferraris for Mike Parkes/Ludovico Scarfiotti, Chris Amon/Nino Vaccarella and Günter Klass/Peter Sutcliffe, not to mention the stellar line-up in the Chaparral, Lola, Matra and Porsche camps or the top privateers, such as Piers Courage/Richard Attwood and Giancarlo Baghetti/Pedro Rodriguez.

Reflecting later on his journey to Le Mans, Nigel Roebuck recalled that 'I was twenty-one years old, newly arrived in London, and *Sgt Pepper's Lonely Hearts Club Band* — released days before the race — was floating around in my head as we went off to France. Life was indeed good in 1967.'

The entire Ferrari team was keen to do as well as possible at Le Mans and hoping to do it in

OPPOSITE LEFT
Dan Gurney celebrates his 1967 Le Mans victory with co-driver A.J. Foyt and establishes the now time-honoured tradition of soaking those closest to the podium with champagne!

OPPOSITE FAR LEFT
Chris Amon motoring quickly through the esses at Le Mans ahead of the Jennings/Johnson Chaparral 2F.

'You can see that virtually anyone with claims to be a serious racing driver was at Le Mans on June 10.'
– Nigel Roebuck

memory of Lorenzo and for his widow Margherita. Indeed it was looking hopeful early in the race and Chris was lying second or third with the other Ferrari of Parkes and Scarfiotti not far behind. 'We were about seven hours into the race, just before midnight, and I'd come past the pits and was going into Dunlop Corner when I felt a bit of a twitch at the rear.' That was bad news but worse was the fact that Chris was at the beginning of the long, fast Mulsanne Straight and there seemed little chance of his making it all the way back to the pits with the suspension upright and the wheel rim grinding along the surface of the road. Accordingly, he pulled off to one side of the straight and got the compact spare tyre, along with a tool kit, out of the engine compartment and set to work.

Eventually, Chris got the jack out and started to crank it up. Having done that, he had to get the hammer, wait for one of the racing cars to come down the straight to give him light, and deliver a smart, accurate blow to the centre-lock spinner, all of which he did. The head of the hammer promptly flew off into the night and landed in the ditch on his side of the track. 'So I'm crawling around in the ditch, looking for the head off this bloody hammer at one in the morning…

'I was obviously going to have to drive it back to the pits somehow so I packed the kit away, got back in, fired up and drove relatively slowly down the straight — but I was probably still doing 100 miles an hour and the tyre was disintegrating, flapping wildly. There were sparks showering back from the suspension upright and I assume that what eventually happened was that a fuel line was knocked off one of the pannier-type fuel tanks just in front of the rear wheels because the whole car just went up in flames!'

While 100 mph was only about half the maximum speed of Chris's Ferrari, it still seemed slow by comparison with the rate at which he had been travelling before the puncture. 'It was getting bloody warm by that stage, so I jumped out thinking I'd almost stopped, but I was probably still doing 50 miles an hour, and I ended up somersaulting down the ditch while the Ferrari rolled another 100 metres along the road before it came to a stop not far from a marshals' post.

'The marshals could see the flames from the car which was now well alight and they came running. There were four of them and three gendarmes and they soon had the fire out and were searching frantically for the driver — me. They were looking around in the ditch wondering where I was, and I remember walking up the ditch, feeling a bit battered, and tapping a gendarme on the shoulder and saying, "Here I am." Poor guy; he bloody nearly died of fright!'

The race would be won by Dan Gurney and A.J. Foyt in a Ford Mark IV from Ludovico Scarfiotti and Mike Parkes and Willy Mairesse and 'Beurlys' in another Ferrari P4, the leading car achieving an average speed of over 135 mph over a distance of 3252 miles.

'There was a sort of jack, a torch and a wheel hammer to knock the centre-lock spinner off. The first thing I discovered was that the batteries in the torch were flat, but there were plenty of cars coming past with their headlights blazing so I had light on and off — occasional illumination at 200 miles per hour.'
– Chris Amon

Brands Hatch, a driver's view

by John Julian with Chris Amon

'Racing at Brands Hatch is a mixed blessing when you've got a place in London because you can get home at night if you want to, but it somehow doesn't feel right because this job is something you normally travel to. The top drivers do a lot of it and all are looking forward to the prospect of supersonic, trans-Atlantic flights courtesy of Concorde in the not-too-distant future. Some still enjoy the relative peace of the cabin of a 707 or a DC8 to catch up with some reading, be it *The Strode Venturer* from Hammond Innes, *Where Eagles Dare* by Alistair MacLean, *The Delta Factor* by Mickey Spillane or simply the latest editions of *Playboy* and *Autosport* or, perhaps, if you're Bruce McLaren, using the time to write a long report for the engineers back at the works.

'The drivers are therefore well-used to long-distance air travel and particularly the trans-Atlantic routes, whether it be the evening flight from London to New York with Pan Am or the equivalent with Trans World or BOAC. Hotels vary from the grandeur of the Villa d'Este near Lake Como to the more modest but no less welcoming Glen Motor Inn, also beside a lake but in upstate New York. Someone once asked whether, as you pause to check that you have all you need for the day ahead, you glance at the bed and wonder whether you will be lying there again tonight or you'll wake up in hospital or not at all.

'Somehow you don't seem to think about that so much in a hotel as you would at home so there's sometimes a more poignant feeling when you leave the house and your belongings for the racetrack, taking the newspaper out of the letterbox, greeting the driver of the early-morning milk float, leaving a saucer of Gold Top by the door for your neighbour's cat as the car warms up and then listening to the rumbling slap of your tyres on the cobblestones as you motor out of the mews and into the street.

THE KLEMANTASKI COLLECTION

'At least you get there in one piece this time, unlike the Thursday before the Race of Champions weekend earlier in the year when you were driving the Sunbeam Tiger and the female currency smuggler ran into you! And so you drive under the circuit through the narrow tunnel near Paddock Bend as usual and park behind the pits and there are the P4s: the one you are sharing with Jackie Stewart, along with the Williams/Hawkins and Scarfiotti/Sutcliffe cars. The Porsche team is fractionally ahead in the World Sports Car Championship but you can clinch it this weekend by finishing in front of them. You hope the team have had a good journey up and that the P4s will be working well at the Kent circuit which is an acquired taste in many ways with adverse camber here, dips and slopes there, a hairpin and a few quick corners.

'You park the car and stroll along the back of the rough row of pit garages towards your own draughty, breezeblock-built box: Phil Hill and Mike Spence are there with the Chaparral, Bruce McLaren and Jo Siffert with the Porsche 910 and Hans Herrmann and Jochen Neerpasch with the sister car. Even in England the weather is fairly reliable at this time of year and as you stop to talk with a good-looking, blue-eyed girl wearing a white sleeveless polo-necked top and trim scarlet shorts with a Ferrari-red cap perched perkily on her pretty blonde head, a cheerful blast on a horn behind you and roars of lewd laughter make you jump. A Ferrari-liveried Ford Transit van containing the Maranello Concessionaires pit crew pulls up alongside you with the Attwood/Piper P3/4 in tow. It's time to go to work!

'The area jokingly known as the Grand Prix paddock behind the pit garages at Brands is woefully small, the garages themselves even more so, and you change in the back of one of the works Ferrari trucks. Accepting a Guards cigarette from one of the Carreras girls, you spend a couple more minutes smoking in the paddock before moving through the dank little garage into the pit lane beyond, which seems more crowded with cars and mechanics, marshals and officials than ever. There's a scrutineer in a tweed jacket with a leather armband looking over your car, kneeling now to peer into a wheel arch, and then he straightens up, catches your eye, nods and smiles and walks on to the next car.

'A man moves in to the gap he's left and applies BOAC Speedbird stickers (the race sponsor's logo) to your car, just behind the door on either side, while a signwriter finishes the black number six he has been painting on the white disc on the nose with a final flourish of his paintbrush. A boy accompanied by his diffident-looking father holds out a programme and a Bic biro and smiles as you sign your name for him. You hear the slick, surgical sound of Nick Loudon's camera shutter and you make a mental note to ask him for a few prints of what you know will be some excellent photographs of the practice and racing action ahead.

'At a signal from your mechanic, you ease yourself into the P4, the car you're sharing with Jackie Stewart today is Chassis 0858 which you drove with Lorenzo to win the 1000-km race at Monza in April and which Willy Mairesse and 'Beurlys' (the pseudonym of a Belgian driver named Jean Blaton) drove at Le Mans, finishing third. It is in Spyder, or open-topped, form for the race this weekend but it has been a coupé, i.e. with a roof, and will eventually be modified to Can-Am configuration for you, and later for Jonathan Williams to race in the last three rounds of that series later in the year.

'But now you motor past the pit lane marshal onto the track, accelerating hard past the Guards and Shell signs, the track rising ahead of you, only to fall again on the approach to Paddock, that curious cambered right-hand descent via an almost invisible apex and then up to the hairpin at Druids, which you can just about take in second before you gather speed going down the hill and drifting through the left-hander, again with adverse camber, and on down the short straight, away to the left and into the country. You'll be taking the car up to almost 170 mph through the trees along this section of the circuit later in the day, but for now you are happy to reacquaint yourself with the P4 as it begins to tramline on the unevenly resurfaced straight. There's not much traffic around, but you still check your mirrors carefully on the way into Hawthorn's Bend and into the second, sharper right-hander at Westfield before accelerating past the Lotus 47 of John Miles and Jackie Oliver, down towards the shallow right and the corner beyond known as Dingle Dell. Through Stirling's Bend, under the bridge and into Clearways, the last, fast corner on the circuit, which takes you back onto the main straight and up to the finishing line about two-thirds of the way along.

'Back in the pits, you talk briefly with David Piper, whose Maranello Concessionnaires' P3 is bottoming badly over the bumps. He has come to seek advice on set-up from the works Ferrari mechanics, who are already busy with your car and the other two P4s. You agree that while they are both fine cars, the P3s and 4s need careful setting up for a Championship that includes circuits as different as Brands Hatch and Le Mans. When the practice session is over, you change out of your overalls and back into the navy polo shirt, tan cotton trousers and Gucci moccasins you put on that morning and you wander across the circuit towards the Grovewood Suite for some lunch.

'Neither Mike Spence nor Phil Hill took any chances the following day, with the latter lapping very cautiously towards the end, even content to stay behind Sutcliffe's Ferrari for several minutes, so he was just one lap ahead of you at the end with the Porsche 910 of Jo Siffert and Bruce McLaren a further lap adrift. Sir Giles Guthrie, Chairman of BOAC, presented the trophies in the calm of that late afternoon. Hap Sharp wore a Texas-sized grin because his giant sports car, the first to feature such a high wing, had won at last.

'On Monday morning you wake up in your bed in London, as you had hoped to do. The difference is that you are now 1967 FIA Group Six World Champion. It was Phil's last race, though, a high point from which to embark upon retirement for the man who won the 1961 Formula One World Championship for Ferrari. The Old Man will be pleased, not least because he has won another World Championship but also because three of his fabulous P4s finished in the top six (second place Amon/Stewart, fifth Scarfiotti/Sutcliffe and sixth Williams/Hawkins) with David Piper and Richard Attwood one place behind that in the Maranello Concessionaires P3/4. It was Franco Lini's birthday, so he was delighted and the mechanics were enjoying themselves too.

'Lying still and listening to London coming to life you realise that Mike, now in hospital, will be cheered by the result, albeit frustrated that he couldn't be part of it, and that poor Lorenzo would have been so happy, not least because you had started the season together and done well. God, you think, it's only the end of July and Daytona was at the beginning of February … six months that feels more like six years in terms of experience. Still, it's better not to dwell on that too much, although maybe we've turned the corner. Now, it's the Nürburgring this weekend so you had better ring up the travel agent and make sure you're booked in at the Sporthotel and find out how you're going to get there. Coffee first, but where on earth is your passport? You'll need that to pick up some more travellers' cheques!'

‘In the meantime, the Commendatore had grown fond of Chris Amon and, taking advantage of this, Chris managed to sell him the idea of competing in the next Can-Am series or, more accurately, the part that took place in the western USA, namely Riverside, Laguna Seca and Las Vegas. I was as delighted as I was surprised when Franco Gozzi informed me that two cars were to be prepared and that one of them would be for me.

‘The cars in question were a pair of re-bodied P4s with wider wheels and the engine capacity stretched to 4.2 litres, and Bill Harrah, the well-known car collector and gambling mogul from Reno, was to be the entrant. We had time for a bare minimum of testing at Modena before the cars were shipped off, which indicated that they were impressively quick in a straight line, but a bit of a handful to drive. Lack of time curtailed any changes being made.’

– Jonathan Williams to John Julian, September 2012

THE KLEMANTASKI COLLECTION

CHAPTER

8

Can-Am

'We had been there in 1965 with Chris and the Ford that was known as "Big Ed". We went to Mosport and to Riverside and on to Nassau Speed Week and that was the forerunner to Can-Am, and I did come back the following year with Peter Revson and Skip Scott. It was a wonderful series because so many people could afford to do it. You could go to Lola or McLaren and buy a car relatively cheaply. There was a lot of prize money around and a privateer could probably make his way if he had a bit of a business, so it was really good racing and there were very big fields.

'About safety; I remember the famous Jackie Stewart story. He went to Laguna Seca and complained about the fact that there were trees too near the track and that they needed to put some Armco barrier there and when he came back he found the Armco behind the trees!'

– Howden Ganley to John Julian, October 2012

Can-Am had emerged during 1966 as a racing series for Fédération International de l'Automobile (FIA) Group Seven cars with unlimited engine capacity and few other technical restrictions, governed by the Sports Car Club of America (SCCA). Supercharging and turbocharging were allowed, aerodynamics were largely left to the designer's imagination; in fact, as long as the car had two seats and a body that enclosed the wheels, and provided it met certain safety standards, it was legal.

The series was also well supported, initially by Johnson's Wax, so both appearance and prize monies made it an attractive proposition for established drivers and constructors. John Surtees won the first Can-Am Championship, which was subsequently nicknamed 'The Bruce and Denny Show' in recognition of the almost crushing domination of Messrs McLaren and Hulme's big orange cars with their thunderous Chevy V8 engines during the last years of Bruce's life. Sadly, he would be killed at Goodwood on 2 June 1970, testing the car he hoped would bring him another Can-Am Championship, when a piece of bodywork became detached and the car slammed into a disused marshal's post.

OPPOSITE
1 September 1967: Chris Amon tests the Can-Am Ferrari 330 P4 Spyder at the Aerautodromo di Modena.

'California, when we got there, was all that I had imagined and more with beautiful weather, fun people and brilliant food ... To add to my already brimming cup of joy, Chick Vandergriff, the Hollywood Ferrari dealer, kindly loaned me a metallic blue 275 GTS for the duration. Life, in a word, was good!'

– Jonathan Williams

GREGG CURRY/SCRAMP ARCHIVES

The series survived in the same form until the end of 1974, when it folded after a last, lacklustre season, a victim of the energy crisis, as much as anything else. It had been immensely popular, with drivers of the calibre of Chris Amon, Jack Brabham, Dan Gurney, David Hobbs, Denny Hulme, Bruce McLaren, Jackie Oliver, Jo Siffert, Jackie Stewart, John Surtees and Jonathan Williams, to mention several whose names appear elsewhere in this book. Among the manufacturers who took advantage of the no-holds-barred nature of the rule book were Ferrari, Lola, McLaren, Porsche and Shadow.

Meanwhile, back in October 1967, Jonathan Williams was getting used to life in California:

'California, when we got there, was all that I had imagined and more with beautiful weather, fun people and brilliant food, by the standards of America then. To add to my already brimming cup of joy, Chick Vandergriff, the Hollywood Ferrari dealer, kindly loaned me a metallic blue 275 GTS for the duration. Life, in a word, was good!

'In the first two races, the Can-Am cars performed predictably enough, considering their lack of development, netting a fifth and eighth place at Laguna Seca and an eighth at Riverside for Chris, when I was forced to retire with a damaged exhaust system incurred in a minor collision. At the final Can-Am race, the so-called "Stardust Grand Prix" held in the desert outside Las Vegas, I was eliminated in a multiple shunt at the first corner of the first lap. Chris crashed on the last corner of the last lap … symmetry we could have done without.'

OPPOSITE
Laguna Seca: Bruce McLaren (4) in pole position from Dan Gurney (36), Denny Hulme (5) and Parnelli Jones (21).

Footnote to the 1967 season

Chris would return to New Zealand in December for the Tasman Series, which started with the New Zealand Grand Prix at Pukekohe on 6 January 1968. This he won, along with the following race at Levin in the Dino-engined Ferrari 246T before Jim Clark recovered his form and won at Wigram in his Lotus 49T with Bruce McLaren taking the round at Teretonga at the end of the month in a BRM P126. The circus then moved to Australia, where Jim Clark won three races and Piers Courage one with the championship going to Clark with 40 points to Amon's 36 and Courage's 34. Graham Hill would finish fourth overall, Denny Hulme seventh equal with Pedro Rodriguez while Jack Brabham scored no points with one seventh place finish and a retirement.

Perhaps the most poignant moment of the series was the podium ceremony after the Australian Grand Prix at Sandown. Jim Clark had just succeeded in beating Chris Amon over the line by the length of a nosecone in what was probably the most exciting finish of the whole Tasman tour. Jack Brabham had started from pole position but Chris had clocked the fastest lap and Graham Hill, in third place, had come in a full minute behind the electrifying Clark-Amon duel. It appeared to be a portent for the 1968 season as a whole but it was not, for Jim Clark had just won his last race and, six weeks later, he would be dead. And just to reinforce the point that the Tasman served as a good guide to contemporary racing form, the overall result was Clark first and Amon second, with four wins to the former and two to the latter; they were two successful farmers' sons from homes about as far from each other as it is physically possible to be on our planet; two boys who had started driving around those farms at a very early age, both of whom had expressed a desire to return to the country when the racing was all over. Sadly, only Chris was able to achieve this — the Grand Prix driver they still call the unlucky one.

There is no doubt that Jim had the better engine for most of 1967 and probably the better chassis too. He was also more experienced than Chris, with two World Championships, 25 wins, 33 pole positions, 28 fastest laps and 274 points scored in 72 Grandes Épreuves contested since the Dutch Grand Prix at Zandvoort in 1960. Very few people brought Jim Clark's brand of artistry, extraordinary sensitivity, courtesy and disarming modesty to the race track, but Chris Amon had many of the same attributes and fortunately he is still with us today.

GRAND PRIX PHOTO

'Was he really unlucky? He drove for two of the top teams in Formula One, he won two of the 24 hour races, he had a wonderful career and he's still here to talk about it. Luck is relative ... he certainly deserved to win the World Championship at least once so from that point of view he was unlucky, but in many other ways he was not.'

– Howden Ganley to John Julian, October 2012

CHAPTER 9

Reflections

'The past is a foreign country: they do things differently there.'
– L.P. Hartley (1895–1972), *The Go-Between*, 1953

'Chris is Chris; he was like a younger brother to me. I still have many happy memories of our dinners together where, over a bottle of Lambrusco, we used to end up singing "Blue Eyes"! We passed many ups and downs in life, but always came through laughing!'
– Brenda Vernor to John Julian, September 2012

Chris Amon would finish fourth equal in the 1967 Drivers' World Championship with John Surtees. The World Champion was Denny Hulme from Te Puke in New Zealand, driving a Brabham-Repco; Hulme was once memorably described by the author Steve Small as 'an unfashionable World Champion; self-effacing to the point of anonymity in his public persona'. He came to Europe in 1960 with George Lawton on the New Zealand Driver to Europe scheme, racing a Cooper in Formula Two and Formula Junior around the Continent. Unfortunately, Lawton was killed at Roskilde Ring, but Denny carried on before returning to contest the Tasman Series early in 1961. While still working as a mechanic at Brabham, Hulme took over the leadership of the Formula Junior team in 1963, winning seven of the 14 races he entered.

In 1965 Brabham had the problem of running himself, Dan Gurney and Denny so he organised the team to ensure that Hulme was well prepared for the three-litre Formula to come. By 1967 it was Hulme's turn in the limelight. His wins at Monaco and at the Nürburgring were outstanding performances, but he scored points consistently and edged out his boss to claim the Drivers' World Championship for himself. Jack Brabham, runner-up in 1967, had won the World Championship in 1959, 1960 and 1966. Still the only driver to win it in a car carrying his name, he was largely responsible for developing the rear-engined Cooper which changed the face of Formula One forever. He was competitive right to the end of his long career, retiring at the age of 44 in 1970, having amassed a total of 261 points including 14 Grand Prix wins from 126 starts.

'He was probably slightly dejected at the end of 1967 because he thought he was going to have the sort of season everybody hopes for and it turned out to be something of a letdown. Chris was a little bit not Chris at that time, but all it took was a pretty girl...'

– Roger Bailey to John Julian, October 2012

'Jim Clark was the only guy that I really felt I could never beat. On my day I felt I could foot it with anybody else but I never felt that Jimmy had to try that hard.'

– Chris Amon to John Julian, June 2012

WWW.FOTOCOMMUNITY.DE

Jim Clark, in third place, had already won the World Championship in 1963 and 1965, both with Team Lotus. Mauro Forghieri believed that Chris was indeed as good as Jim Clark but that in 312/67, he had not delivered a racing car in which Chris could consistently beat his Scottish rival. Fabulous to behold, sleek and scarlet, with golden wheels and a white-painted, Medusa-like tangle of exhaust pipes between the cylinder heads, which emitted a joyful howl at high revs and delighted all within earshot, 312/67, while a pleasure to handle, was not quite powerful enough to run with the new Cosworth DFV-engined Lotus 49 until the 48-valve version of the Ferrari V12 made its debut at Monza. Chris Amon and Jim Clark shared more than a talent for extracting the maximum velocity, however, for both were born into prosperous farming families at opposite ends of the world and it is fair to speculate that the driving they did on the family properties, long before they had a licence for the road, meant that their instinctive car control became as natural as any skill honed from an early age, which allowed them more time to refine the artistry of speed, of which they were two well-recognised masters at the time.

Tragically, Jim Clark would die in a Formula Two race at Hockenheim on 7 April 1968. It was one of those eerie days at the German circuit with a light rain falling and the spray from the cars seemingly suspended around the trees like layers of fog. Clark's Lotus left the circuit, probably due to suspension failure, although other potential causes have been suggested and thoroughly investigated, and the car hit a tree. There was no safety barrier. Jim Clark would remain one of the truly great drivers of any era and his loss was akin to that of Ayrton Senna in 1994 for both drivers set the benchmark for their peers with performances that were often truly extraordinary and on a different plane. As Dan Gurney had observed three years before Clark died, 'Racing drivers usually try to spot weaknesses in each other. Offhand I can't think of any in Jim.'

Another of Chris's rivals that year was John Surtees, the only man to have won World Championships on motorcycles as well as in racing cars. John remains enormously popular to this day among fans of both disciplines, not least in Italy. He won seven World Championships on two wheels for MV Agusta between 1956 and 1960 and was World Champion on four for Ferrari in 1964. He started 111 races, won 6 and scored a total of 180 points.

The Mexican Pedro Rodriguez finished one place behind Chris Amon in the 1967 points total. The Mexican had driven for Lotus, NART, Ferrari, Cooper, BRM and Scuderia Ferrari during a career that spanned 55 Grands Prix, of which he won 2 and scored 71 points. An expert sports car driver, he would win Le Mans in 1968 with Lucien Bianchi in John Wyer's Ford GT40, and he drove for both Ferrari and Matra the following year before returning to Wyer in 1970. In 1971 he was victorious at Daytona, Monza and Spa with Jack Oliver and at the Österreichring 1000 km with Richard Attwood, but it was in Herbert Mueller's Ferrari 512M that he crashed heavily after a tyre deflated and he died in the car on the afternoon of 11 July at the Norisring, close to Nuremberg in Germany.

Graham Hill lay seventh at the end of the year, the 1962 World Champion having amassed a total of 15 points to add to his eventual career total of 289, including 14 wins from 176 starts. Had the Lotus 49-Ford been a little more reliable, he would undoubtedly have done better, but he would use it to earn another World Championship before his retirement and subsequent death in an air accident near Elstree in England during November 1975.

Dan Gurney is a driver and constructor whose Formula One career had begun with Scuderia Ferrari in 1959. He would go on to drive for BRM, Porsche, Brabham, his own Anglo-American Racers organisation and for Bruce McLaren before

COURTESY OF THE HONDA MOTOR COMPANY

ABOVE
10 September 1967: John Surtees wins the 1967 Italian Grand Prix by 0.2 seconds from Jack Brabham. The new Honda RA300 V12 was competing in its first Grand Prix.

OPPOSITE
1967: no six-point harness, no full-face helmet and sharp edges in and around the cockpit. Things would eventually start to improve, but not for a year or so.

retiring from Grand Prix motor racing in 1970. Of 86 Grands Prix entered, he won 4, also taking 3 pole positions and 6 fastest laps for a total of 133 points. He continues to run the very successful All American Racers Inc in Santa Ana, California.

Jackie Stewart, lying in ninth place, is another reminder of the supreme quality of the field that Chris Amon faced during the 1967 season. He had already partnered Chris in a Ferrari sports car and there had been rumours to the effect that he would join Amon at Ferrari for the 1968 Formula One season, but the drive would eventually go to Jacky Ickx. Stewart would win an amazing total of 27 races and gain 17 pole positions and 15 fastest laps from 99 Grand Prix starts between 1965 and 1973 and he would be World Champion in 1969, 1971 and 1973. He would have completed 100 Grands Prix had it not been for the death

NICK LOUDON

LEFT
The superlative P4 with which Chris Amon and Lorenzo Bandini won at Daytona and again at Monza before Lorenzo was killed during the Monaco Grand Prix. Chris then finished second at Brands Hatch with Jackie Stewart on 30 July, thereby clinching the 1967 FIA Group Six World Championship.

OPPOSITE
Arguably the best photograph ever taken of Chris Amon in action, albeit in 1968, this is Nick Loudon's matchless study of Chris drifting his Ferrari on the throttle with a touch of opposite lock to maintain the optimum line through Old Hall Corner at Oulton Park (UK) on 17 August during the annual Gold Cup meeting. He would finish second, between Jackie Stewart's winning Matra and Jackie Oliver's third-placed Lotus. Very few drivers have ever exhibited such an apparently effortless blend of artistry and car control, style and mechanical sympathy at this level.

at Watkins Glen in 1973 of his young French teammate, François Cevert but, like Chris, he would emerge unscathed from the fray to bear living witness to the dangerous days of the 1960s, when he led the charge to improve driver safety in Grand Prix and other forms of motor sport.

Tenth in the tables in 1967 was Mike Spence, Stewart's teammate at BRM. His had been a long haul to the top and his first Grand Prix had taken place four years earlier when he contested the Italian event at Monza in a 1.5-litre Lotus 25-Climax V8 and by 1967 he was driving the H16 BRM alongside Jackie Stewart. This was a complicated and troublesome car and he did very well to bring it to five points finishes. 1968 looked very promising for Mike and he was about to reinforce his reputation among the very top echelon of Grand Prix drivers. The shadow of Jim Clark, which had inevitably held him back at Lotus, would pass over him once more as he took the late Scotsman's place for the Indianapolis 500 in 1968. In qualifying everything went well, but when Spence took a teammate's car out for a few shakedown laps, he lost control and crashed into the wall. The right front wheel flew back and struck his head and he died in hospital a few hours later.

NICK LOUDON

It is sobering to consider that of the Top Ten of 1967 only Jack Brabham, John Surtees, Chris Amon, Dan Gurney and Jackie Stewart remain alive. It is equally thought-provoking to reflect that of the other drivers, Jochen Rindt, Jo Siffert, Bruce McLaren, Jo Bonnier and Bob Anderson all had their lives curtailed because of the sport they loved. Furthermore, Mike Parkes and Chris Irwin were injured to the point where they could no longer drive Grand Prix cars. With Ludovico Scarfiotti later killed in an accident while driving a Porsche and John Love dying in 2005 aged 80, of all those who started a Grand Prix during 1967 (including Formula Two drivers), only Kurt Ahrens, Jean-Pierre Beltoise, Dave Charlton, Mike Fisher, Hubert Hahne, Brian Hart, David Hobbs, Jacky Ickx, Guy Ligier, Jackie Oliver, Al Pease, Alan Rees, Eppie Wietzes and Jonathan Williams, in addition to those mentioned earlier, are left at the time of writing. It is a small club made up of brave men who raced at a very different time.

'It is the only sport I know that can engender such a varied range of emotions. At one moment it is cruelly beautiful ... a lone blood-red Ferrari sweeping through the sand-dunes of the Dutch coast, making the pulse leap with wonder ... and then, suddenly, and inexplicably, it can be fantastically grotesque as when a driver all the world knows ends his life dramatically in a mass of twisted metal and burning rubber, the crowd staring blankly and silently – and the track marshals waving their multi-coloured flags in their strangely surrealistic form of epitaph, like a mediaeval death-rite.'

– Michael Frewin, Editor, *The International Book of Grand Prix Motor Racing*, 1965

THE KLEMANTASKI COLLECTION

CHAPTER 10

Postscript ... Why?

Izo Yamura: 'Why do you drive racing cars, or do you not think about it?'

Pete Aron: 'Oh, Mr Yamura, I don't think there's one of us who doesn't ask himself at least once in the middle of a race, "What the hell am I doing here?" Of course, when it's over, we conveniently forget that we asked ourselves that question. I think about it and a lot of reasons I don't know. Maybe to do something that brings you so close to the possibility of death and to survive it is to feel life and living so much more intensely.'

– Pete Aron (James Garner) talking with team principal Izo Namura (Toshiro Mifune) during John Frankenheimer's 1966 movie *Grand Prix*

OPPOSITE
7 May 1967: Chris Amon drives past the blazing wreck of his teammate's car. Lorenzo Bandini would die later that week from the injuries he sustained in the crash. Bandini's hideous and widely publicised accident would have far-reaching and positive effects upon a sport that was taking many lives. Motor racing remains dangerous, but mercifully such tragedies as this one are now fewer and further between.

C'était plus fort que lui is hard to translate. 'He couldn't resist it' is a fair approximation; 'It was too strong for him' comes closer, but perhaps 'He couldn't help himself' is nearer still. It's a phrase that could be used to illustrate the emotional intensity, the sheer passion that some men feel for motor racing, occasionally with tragic consequences. It can result in death or serious injury, a broken marriage or financial ruin, but anyone who has competed in a motor race of any consequence is vulnerable. There is no particular antidote to this often overpowering sensation and, of course, the affliction is contagious.

There are cooler heads in the business of motor sport too, although most team principals find it hard to be totally detached from the racing. The sponsors' view is obviously more clinical in 2013 than it was during 1967, long before media exposures became a form of currency, but while the advent of big money has made motor sport somewhat safer and has turned Formula One into the matchless marketing machine it is today, it has also diminished the quixotic, sometimes eccentric charm that was part of the game in the sixties. Fortunately, however, the risk of a driver dying or being badly injured has also been reduced during this time.

Jean-Pierre Sarti: 'I've begun to see the absurdity of it. All of us, proving what? That we can go faster, and perhaps remain alive... Don't you see how absurd it all is? Who cares?'

Louise Frederickson: 'I thought you cared, for yourselves. I didn't know you asked of anyone else. Nevertheless, others do care. One hundred thousand of them cared today.'

Jean-Pierre Sarti: 'And did you see them rush to see Peter burn? Did you see the looks on their faces? I saw. For the first time today I really saw those faces.'

Louise Frederickson: 'But not all of them, Jean-Pierre. There are some that come for that, for the accidents and the fires. But the others ... the others ride with you all. You put something in their lives they can't put there themselves.'

– Jean-Pierre Sarti (Yves Montand) talking with Louise Frederickson (Eva Marie Saint) during John Frankenheimer's 1966 movie *Grand Prix*

As Henry Ford once observed: 'Auto racing began five minutes after the second car was built.' The human race always has been competitive, from running and riding to driving and flying, and something in our mental make-up means that we have to find out where the limits are. The best of the racing drivers and fighter pilots, athletes and jockeys live on that edge most of the time and the rest of us like going to see how they do it. We can take vicarious pleasure in watching the New Zealander put his Ferrari on pole with one searing lap or the Frenchman ride his thoroughbred to victory by a short head, even if we can't share the heights of consciousness brought on by the coursing adrenalin and the sweet self-congratulation that comes when the winner acknowledges the cheering crowds. There is no substitute for that.

THE KLEMANTASKI COLLECTION

'There is a kind of compulsion. Grand Prix drivers don't know what it is and nor, so far as I can discover, can anyone else give a totally convincing explanation.'
– Richard Garrett, *Anatomy of a Grand Prix Driver*, 1970

'Motor racing also comes up in the same breath with boxing and bullfighting under the topic of blood sports. However, there is one essential difference: the allure of the first two seems based on the promise of bloodletting, whereas the opposite is true in motor racing. It is not the promise of bodily harm but, vicariously or in actuality, the exhilaration of returning unscathed from an excursion into a realm where life hangs most delicately in the balance. You only have to witness the reaction of the people in a crowd to a fatal accident — intense depression at this affirmation of their own mortality — to know the truth of this.'
– Charles Fox, *The Great Racing Cars and Drivers*, 1972

'There really isn't that much that need be said about this subject beyond what you see in the photos. Regardless of what anyone has to say about the drivers, cars or the racing circuits, the sport of automobile racing will continue to be a matter of human beings all tied up facing an ultimate contest over the course of a weekend, sometimes winning, usually losing and, for an unfortunate few, dying.'
– Phil Hill, *The Automotive Photography of Peter Coltrin*, 1978

OPPOSITE
25 April 1967: Chris Amon climbs on board the Ferrari 330 P4 he co-drove with Lorenzo Bandini at Monza. They won, as they had at the 24 Hour Race at Daytona on 5 February.

'This will make you crazy in this day of political correctness, but the element of danger — and yes, even death — remains the differential between Hemingway's three sports and children's games. Some critics of racing witlessly claim that spectators only attend to see someone die. This is utter and complete nonsense. I have been at numerous races where death is present. When a driver dies, the crowd symbolically dies too. They come to see action at the brink: ultimate risk taking and the display of skill and bravery embodied in the sport's immortals like Nuvolari, Foyt, and thousands of others who operate at the ragged edge.'
– Brock Yates, author of *Enzo Ferrari*, 1991, at www.caranddriver.com/columns/hemingway-wouldn't-recognize-it-today/ October 2005

'These episodes seem unthinkable from the perspective of today's risk-averse culture. Formula One cars are now so safe that more than a decade passes between fatalities. But even today, there are still some who believe, as [Count Wolfgang] von Trips did, that it is danger and the insistent proximity to death that most ennobles the soul.'
– Michael Cannell, *The Limit*, 2011

'Faster, faster until the thrill of speed overcomes the fear of death.'
– Hunter S. Thompson (date unknown).

Appendix One: 1967 results

Sports prototype title races contested by works Ferrari drivers during 1967

Daytona Beach Raceway USA, 4–5 February 1967

1 Bandini/Amon (Ferrari 330 P4), 666 laps, 2537 miles, 105.73 mph
2 Scarfiotti/Parkes (Ferrari 330 P4), 663 laps
3 Rodriguez/Guichet (Ferrari 330 P4), 637 laps
4 Herrmann/Siffert (Porsche 910), 618 laps
5 van Lennep/Schutz/Stommelen (Porsche 910), 608 laps
6 Thompson/Ickx (Ford GT40), 601 laps

Fastest lap: Phil Hill (Chaparral-Chevrolet 2F), 1 min 55.7 sec, 122.67 mph

Monza 1000 km, Italy, 25 April 1967

1 Bandini/Amon (Ferrari 330 P4), 100 laps, 1000 km, 5 hrs 7 min 43 sec, 122.369 mph
2 Scarfiotti/Parkes (Ferrari 330 P4), 5 hrs 10 min 59.2 sec
3 Mitter/Rindt (Porsche 910), 96 laps
4 Vaccarella/Muller (Ferrari P3/4), 95 laps
5 Hermann/Siffert (Porsche 910), 95 laps
6 Schlesser/Ligier (Ford GT40), 95 laps

Fastest lap: Chris Amon (Ferrari 330 P4), 2 min 55.8 sec, 128.516 mph

Spa 1000 km, Belgium, 1 May 1967

1 Ickx/Thompson (Mirage), 71 laps, 1000 km, 5 hrs 9 min 46.5 sec
2 Herrmann/Siffert (Porsche 910), 70 laps
3 Bianchi/Attwood (Ferrari 330 P4), 70 laps
4 Hawkins/Epstein (Lola-Chevrolet T70 Mark 3 GT), 69 laps
5 Scarfiotti/Parkes (Ferrari 330 P4), 69 laps
6 Sutcliffe/Redman (Ford P40), 68 laps

Fastest lap: Phil Hill (Chaparral-Chevrolet 2F), 4 min 3.5 sec, 146.277 mph

Targa Florio, Madonie Circuit, Sicily, 14 May 1967

1 Hawkins/Stommelen (2.2 Porsche 910), 10 laps, 450 miles, 6 hrs 37 min 01 sec, 67.46 mph
2 Cella/Biscaldi (2.0 Porsche 910)
3 Neerpasch/Elford (2.0 Porsche 910)
4 Williams/Venturi (Ferrari Dino)
5 Greder/Giorgi (Ford GT40)
6 Herrmann/Siffert (2.2 Porsche 910)

Nürburgring 1000 km, Germany, 28 May 1967

1 Schutz/Buzzetta (2.0 Porsche 910), 44 laps, 1000 km, 6 hrs 54 min 12.9 sec, 90.2 mph

2 Hawkins/Koch (2.0 Porsche 910)
3 Neerpasch/Elford (2.0 Porsche 910)
4 Mitter/Bianchi (2.2 Porsche 910)
5 de Adamich/Galli/Bussinello/Zeccoli (Alfa Romeo T33)
6 Dechent/Huhn (Porsche 906)

Fastest lap: P. Hill (Chaparral-Chevrolet 2F), 8 min 42.1 sec, 94.4 mph

Le Mans 24 Hours, France, 10–11 June 1967

1 Gurney/Foyt (Ford GT Mk 4), 3251.7 miles, 135.483 mph
2 Scarfiotti/Parkes (Ferrari 330 P4), 3217.146 miles
3 Mairesse/'Beurlys' (Ferrari 330 P4), 3157.306 miles
4 McLaren/Donohue (Ford GT Mk 4), 3008.211 miles
5 Siffert/Herrmann (2.0 Porsche 910), 2999.772 miles
6 Stommelen/Neerpasch (2.0 Porsche), 2940.994 miles

Fastest lap: Denny Hulme and Mario Andretti (Ford GT Mk 4s), 3 min 23.6 sec, 147.894 mph

International BOAC 500, Brands Hatch, 30 July 1967

1 P. Hill/Spence (Chaparral-Chevrolet), 211 laps, 6 hrs 00 min 26.0 sec, 93.08 mph
2 Amon/Stewart (Ferrari 330 P4), 211 laps in 6 hrs 1 min 24.6 sec
3 Siffert/McLaren (2.2 Porsche 910), 209 laps
4 Herrmann/Neerpasch (2.2 Porsche 910), 206 laps
5 Scarfiotti/Sutcliffe (Ferrari 330 P4), 206 laps
6 Williams/Hawkins (Ferrari 330 P4), 204 laps

Can-Am races contested by works Ferrari drivers during 1967

Canadian-American Challenge Cup Round 4; Monterey Grand Prix, Laguna Seca Raceway, 15 October 1967

1 Bruce McLaren (McLaren-Chevrolet M6A), 106 laps, 1 hr 58 min 55.8 sec
2 Jim Hall (Chaparral-Chevrolet 2G), 105 laps
3 George Follmer (Lola-Chevrolet T70 Mk 3), 104 laps
4 Bud Morley (Lola-Chevrolet T70 Mk 3), 103, laps
5 Chris Amon (Ferrari 330 P4), 102 laps
6 Bill Eve (Lola-Chevrolet T70 Mk 3), 101 laps

Fastest lap: Bruce McLaren (McLaren-Chevrolet M6A), 1 min 4.7 sec

Canadian-American Challenge Cup Round 5; Los Angeles Times Grand Prix, Riverside International Raceway, 29 October 1967

1 Bruce McLaren (McLaren-Chevrolet M6A), 62 laps, 1 hr 46 min 7.0 sec
2 Jim Hall (Chaparral-Chevrolet 2G), 62 laps, 1 hr 46 min 32 sec
3 Mark Donohue (Lola T70-Chevrolet Mk 3B), 61 laps
4 Parnelli Jones (Lola T70-Ford Mk 3), 61 laps
5 Mike Spence (McLaren-Elva-Chevrolet Mark II), 61 laps
6 George Follmer (Lola T70-Chevrolet Mk 3), 60 laps

Fastest lap: Bruce McLaren (McLaren-Chevrolet M6A), 1 min 40.4 sec

Canadian-American Challenge Cup Round 6; Third Annual Stardust Grand Prix, Stardust International Raceway, Las Vegas, 12 November 1967

1 John Surtees (Lola T70-Chevrolet Mk 2), 70 laps, 1 hr 52 min 5.5 sec
2 Mark Donohue (Lola T70-Chevrolet Mk 3B), 70 laps, 1 hr 52 min 17.5 sec
3 Mike Spence (McLaren-Elva-Chevrolet Mark II), 70 laps, 1 hr 52 min 41.5 sec
4 Charlie Hayes (McKee-Oldsmobile Mk 7), 69 laps
5 Bud Morley (Lola T70-Chevrolet Mk 3), 66 laps
6 Rick Muther (Lola T70-Chevrolet Mk 2), 65 laps

Fastest lap: Denny Hulme (McLaren Chevrolet M6A), 1 min 32.5 sec

International Formula One races contested by works Ferrari drivers (non-championship)

Race of Champions, Brands Hatch, 12 March 1967

Heat One, 10 laps, 26.5 miles:

1 Dan Gurney (Eagle Gurney-Weslake V12)
2 John Surtees (Honda)

3 Richie Ginther (Eagle Gurney-Weslake V12)
4 Bruce McLaren (2-litre McLaren BRM)
5 Mike Spence (BRM H-16)
6 Ludovico Scarfiotti (Ferrari)

Heat Two, 10 laps, 26.5 miles:

1 Dan Gurney (Eagle Gurney-Weslake V12)
2 Richie Ginther (Eagle Gurney-Weslake V12)
3 John Surtees (Honda)
4 Ludovico Scarfiotti (Ferrari)
5 Pedro Rodriguez (Cooper-Maserati)
6 Bruce McLaren (2-litre McLaren-BRM)

Final, 40 laps, 106 miles:

1 Dan Gurney (Eagle Gurney-Weslake V12), 1 hr 4 min 30.6 sec, 98.66 mph
2 Lorenzo Bandini (Ferrari), 1 hr 4 min 31.0 sec
3 Jo Siffert (Cooper-Maserati), 1 hr 4 min 32.6 sec
4 Pedro Rodriguez (Cooper-Maserati), 1 hr 4 min 33.4 sec
5 Ludovico Scarfiotti (Ferrari), 1 hr 4 min 34.8 sec
6 Chris Irwin (2-litre Lotus-BRM), 39 laps

Fastest lap: Jack Brabham (Repco-Brabham), 1 min 34.4 sec, 101.06 mph

International Daily Express Trophy, Silverstone, 29 April 1967, 52 laps, 152 miles

1 Mike Parkes (Ferrari), 1 hr 19 min 39.2 sec, 114.65 mph
2 Jack Brabham (Repco-Brabham), 1 hr 19 min 56.8 sec
3 Jo Siffert (Cooper-Maserati), 1 hr 19 min 57.6 sec
4 Graham Hill (2-litre Lotus-BRM), 1 hr 19 min 58.0 sec
5 Bruce McLaren (2-litre McLaren-BRM)
6 Mike Spence (2-litre BRM)

Fastest lap: Graham Hill (2-litre Lotus-BRM), 1 min 30.0 sec, 117.08 mph

Syracuse Grand Prix, 21 May 1967, 56 laps, 200 miles

1= Dead heat between Mike Parkes (Ferrari) and Ludovico Scarfiotti (Ferrari), 1 hr 40 min 58.4 sec, 115.47 mph
3 Jo Siffert (Cooper-Maserati), 54 laps
4 Chris Irwin (2-litre Lotus BRM), 53 laps
5 Jo Bonnier (Cooper-Maserati), 53 laps

Fastest lap: Ludovico Scarfiotti (Ferrari), 1 min 41.0 sec, 121.82 mph (new record)

Grands Prix contested by works Ferrari drivers (World Championship) during 1967

25th Monaco Grand Prix, Monaco, 7 May 1967, 100 laps, 195 miles

1 Denny Hulme (Repco-Brabham), 2 hrs 34 min 34.3 sec, 75.90 mph
2 Graham Hill (1.9-litre Lotus-BRM V8), 99 laps
3 Chris Amon (Ferrari), 98 laps
4 Bruce McLaren (2-litre McLaren-BRM V8), 97 laps
5 Pedro Rodriguez (Cooper-Maserati), 96 laps
6 Mike Spence (BRM H16), 96 laps

Fastest lap: Jim Clark (2-litre Lotus-Climax V8), 1 min 29.5 sec, 78.6 mph (new record)

17th Dutch Grand Prix, Zandvoort, 4 June 1967, 90 laps, 234.5 miles

1 Jim Clark (Lotus-Ford), 2 hrs 14 min 45.1 sec, 104.4 mph
2 Jack Brabham (Repco-Brabham), 2 hrs 15 min 8.7 sec
3 Denny Hulme (Repco-Brabham), 2 hrs 15 min 10.8 sec
4 Chris Amon (Ferrari), 2 hrs 15 min 12.4 sec
5 Mike Parkes (Ferrari), 89 laps
6 Ludovico Scarfiotti (Ferrari), 89 laps

Fastest lap: Jim Clark (Lotus-Ford), 1 min 28.08 sec, 106.49 mph (new record)

27th Belgian Grand Prix, Spa-Francorchamps, 18 June 1967, 28 laps, 245 miles

1 Dan Gurney (Eagle Gurney-Weslake V12), 1 hr 40 min 49.4 sec, 145.98 mph
2 Jackie Stewart (BRM H16), 1 hr 41 min 52.4 sec
3 Chris Amon (Ferrari), 1 hr 42 min 29.4 sec
4 Jochen Rindt (Cooper-Maserati), 1 hr 43 min 3.3 sec
5 Mike Spence (BRM H16), 27 laps
6 Jim Clark (Lotus-Ford), 27 laps

Fastest lap: Dan Gurney (Eagle Gurney-Weslake V12), 3 min 31.9 sec, 148.85 mph (new record)

53rd French Grand Prix, Le Mans, 2 July 1967, 80 laps, 219 miles

1 Jack Brabham (Repco-Brabham), 2 hrs 13 min 21.3 sec, 98.90 mph
2 Denny Hulme (Repco-Brabham), 2 hrs 14 min 10.8 sec
3 Jackie Stewart (2.1-litre BRM), 79 laps
4 Jo Siffert (Cooper-Maserati), 77 laps
5 Chris Irwin (BRM H16), 76 laps
6 Pedro Rodriguez (Cooper-Maserati), 76 laps

Fastest lap: Graham Hill (Lotus Ford), 1 min 36.7 sec, 102.297 mph (new record)

20th British Grand Prix, Silverstone, 15 July 1967, 80 laps, 240 miles

1 Jim Clark (Lotus-Ford), 1 hr 59 min 25.6 sec, 117.64 mph
2 Denny Hulme (Repco-Brabham), 1 hr 59 min 38.4 sec
3 Chris Amon (Ferrari), 1 hr 59 min 42.2 sec
4 Jack Brabham (Repco-Brabham), 1 hr 59 min 47.4 sec
5 Pedro Rodriguez (Cooper-Maserati), 79 laps
6 John Surtees (Honda), 78 laps

Fastest lap: Denny Hulme (Repco-Brabham), 1 min 27.0 sec, 121.12 mph (new record)

29th German Grand Prix, Nürburgring, 6 August 1967, 15 laps, 213 miles

1 Denny Hulme (Repco-Brabham), 2 hrs 5 min 55.7 sec, 101.47 mph
2 Jack Brabham (Repco-Brabham), 2 hrs 6 min 34.2 sec
3 Chris Amon (Ferrari), 2 hrs 6 min 34.7 sec
4 John Surtees (Honda), 2 hrs 8 min 21.4 sec
5 Jackie Oliver (Lotus-Cosworth 48), 2 hrs 12 min 4.9 sec
6 Jo Bonnier (Cooper-Maserati), 2 hrs 14 min 37.8 sec

Fastest lap: Dan Gurney (Eagle Gurney-Weslake V12), 8 min 15.1 sec, 103.15 mph (new record)

1st Canadian Grand Prix, Mosport Park, 27 August 1967, 90 laps, 221 miles

1 Jack Brabham (Repco-Brabham), 2 hrs 40 min 0 sec, 82.65 mph
2 Denny Hulme (Repco-Brabham), 2 hrs 41 min 41.9 sec
3 Dan Gurney (Eagle Gurney-Weslake V12), 89 laps
4 Graham Hill (Lotus-Ford), 88 laps
5 Mike Spence (BRM H16), 87 laps
6 Chris Amon (Ferrari), 87 laps

Fastest lap: Jim Clark (Lotus-Ford), 1 min 23.1 sec, 106.53 mph

38th Italian Grand Prix, Monza, 10 September 1967, 68 laps, 243 miles

1 John Surtees (Honda), 1 hr 43 min 45.0 sec, 140.50 mph
2 Jack Brabham (Repco-Brabham), 1 hr 43 min 45.2 sec
3 Jim Clark (Lotus-Ford), 1 hr 44 min 8.1 sec
4 Jochen Rindt (Cooper-Maserati), 1 hr 44 min 41.6 sec
5 Mike Spence (BRM H16), 67 laps
6 Jacky Ickx (Cooper-Maserati), 66 laps

Fastest lap: Jim Clark (Lotus-Ford), 1 min 28.5 sec, 145.34 mph (new record)

9th United States Grand Prix, Watkins Glen, 1 October 1967, 108 laps, 248 miles

1 Jim Clark (Lotus-Ford), 2 hrs 3 min 13.2 sec, 120.95 mph

2 Graham Hill (Lotus-Ford), 2 hrs 3 min 19.5 sec

3 Denny Hulme (Repco-Brabham), 107 laps

4 Jo Siffert (Cooper-Maserati), 106 laps

5 Jack Brabham (Repco-Brabham), 104 laps

6 Jo Bonnier (Cooper-Maserati), 101 laps

Fastest lap: Graham Hill (Lotus-Ford), 1 min 6.0 sec, 125.455 mph (new record)

6th Mexican Grand Prix, Mexico City, 22 October, 65 laps, 202 miles

1 Jim Clark (Lotus-Ford), 1 hr 59 min 28.70 sec, 101.42 mph

2 Jack Brabham (Repco-Brabham), 2 hrs 00 min 54.06 sec

3 Denny Hulme (Repco-Brabham), 64 laps

4 John Surtees (Honda), 64 laps

5 Mike Spence (BRM H16), 63 laps

6 Pedro Rodriguez (Cooper-Maserati), 63 laps

Fastest lap: Jim Clark (Lotus-Ford), 1 min 48.13 sec, 103.44 mph (new record)

1967 Drivers' World Championship points

1	Denny Hulme, Repco-Brabham:	51
2	Jack Brabham, Repco-Brabham:	46
3	Jim Clark, Lotus-Ford:	41
4	Chris Amon, Ferrari:	20
5	John Surtees, Honda:	20
6	Pedro Rodriguez, Cooper-Maserati:	15
7	Graham Hill, Lotus-Ford:	15
8	Dan Gurney, Eagle Gurney-Weslake V12:	13
9	Jackie Stewart, BRM:	10
10	Mike Spence, BRM:	9
11	John Love, Cooper-Climax:	6
12	Jochen Rindt, Cooper-Maserati:	6
13	Jo Siffert, Cooper-Maserati:	6
14	Jo Bonnier, Cooper-Maserati:	3
15	Bruce McLaren, McLaren-BRM:	3
16	Chris Irwin, BRM:	2
17	Mike Parkes, Ferrari:	2
18	Jacky Ickx, Cooper-Maserati:	1
19	Guy Ligier, Repco-Brabham:	1
20	Ludovico Scarfiotti, Ferrari:	1

Appendix Two

A: Manetta-Ferrari and the movie *Grand Prix*

The young American movie director John Frankenheimer made what many still consider the ultimate motor racing screen epic in 1966 during the course of a campaign that saw some 200 people moved across six countries in five months. With a budget of US$10 million (in 1966 money) Frankenheimer, backed by producer Edward Lewis and the might of Metro-Goldwyn-Mayer, moved from Monaco to Monza through Belgium, England, Holland and France buying cars and commissioning replicas, which were filmed at the circuits concerned. The cast included actors of the calibre of Yves Montand and James Garner, Oscar-winner Eva Marie Saint and Jessica Walter.

John Frankenheimer also engaged real Grand Prix drivers, such as Chris Amon, Bruce McLaren and Phil Hill. These men would drive instead of the actors Yves Montand, Brian Bedford and Antonio Sabato. James Garner did most of his own driving, much to the horror of insurers at Lloyd's of London, which prompted Richie Ginther to comment approvingly that 'he drives like a pro and talks like a mechanic'. Enzo Ferrari, while initially reluctant to offer his assistance, watched many hours of Frankenheimer's filming and, once convinced it was a serious production, extended his cooperation to both the director and those playing the parts of the Manetta-Ferrari team personnel. *Andare a manetta* means to drive flat out, so the name of the famous but semi-fictitious Formula One team led on screen by the Italian actor Adolfo Celi translates roughly as Flat Out Ferrari!

Chris Amon also drove a camera-carrying Ford GT40, which could tow the studio's single-seaters at speeds of up to 130 mph, while filming the cars and their actor-drivers. As an acknowledged sports car expert and winner of that year's Le Mans 24 Hour Race, Chris was able to demonstrate the art of high-performance driving, not just to the onboard cameraman or director, but also to an actor travelling at over two miles per minute in what was effectively a two-wheeled trailer!

B: Reg Parnell Racing, Yeoman Credit and the Samengo-Turner family

Yeoman Credit, a British finance company that was owned and run by the Samengo-Turner family until it was sold to Bowmaker, was the first commercial sponsor, as opposed to supplier, in motor racing to use a livery or colours as a means of advertising. The team was managed by Reg Parnell and ran Formula One Coopers and Lolas under the Yeoman Credit, Bowmaker and Reg Parnell (Racing) banners for such drivers as Chris Bristow, Roy Salvadori, John Surtees and Chris Amon between 1960 and 1963. Chris joined the team in April 1963, replacing John Surtees, who had left for Ferrari, with which he would win the World Championship the following year. Chris Amon's first two Formula One races were at Goodwood and Aintree; he would finish fifth and sixth and *Motor Racing* magazine's reporter noted that at both circuits 'The young New Zealander Chris Amon showed a consistency and a lack of flamboyance which belies his youth (he is only 19 years of age), and that Reg Parnell has found a useful recruit for his ex-Bowmaker Lola-Climax'. Chris would eventually take John Surtees' place at Ferrari after the latter fell out with Eugenio Dragoni in the summer of 1966.

Acknowledgements

Chris Amon, Jonathan Williams, John Surtees, Dan and Evi Gurney, Jackie Oliver, David Hobbs, Howden Ganley, Eva Marie Saint, Sue Goold, Peter Gaydon, Brenda Vernor, Roger Bailey, Paul-Henri Cahier, Peter Sachs, Nick Loudon, Peter Nygaard, Michael Turner, Annabel Parkes Campigotto, Johnnie Parkes, Tony Willis, Nicky Samengo-Turner, Nick Paterson-Morgan, Alan Campbell, John Glover, Steve Bryan, the late Bill Jupe, the late Gerald Lascelles, the late Innes Ireland, and the late Johnny Servoz-Gavin.

Nigel Roebuck, Eoin Young, Bob Constanduros, Gerald Donaldson, Maurice Hamilton, Alan Henry, Andrew Marriott, Peter Windsor and the late Richard Garrett.

Julie McDermid, Brian O'Flaherty at Punaromia Publications in Auckland and Donna Vincent and the team at Workz4u in Pukekohe.

Many other people have contributed to this book in all sorts of ways, which has made the project even more enjoyable, and I hope I have remembered to thank everyone concerned for their words and pictures, suggestions and ideas. Any oversights are unintentional and are my responsibility alone.

There is one charismatic and determined individual without whose life and work there could have been no such story, however. Enzo Anselmo Ferrari's birth remained unregistered for a couple of days, due to a snowstorm near Modena, but it was on or about 18 February 1898. He died close by on 14 August 1988, and his legacy transcends the art and science of road and racing car production.

'I can clearly remember the words [Ferrari] said to me not long before he died. "John, let us remember the good times and not the mistakes."'

John Surtees, Ferrari Grand Prix driver (1963–66) and World Champion (1964)

Photo Credits

Paul-Henri Cahier and the Cahier Archive; Peter Sachs and the Klemantaski Collection; Nick Loudon; Gregg Curry, Archivist at SCRAMP (The Sports Car Racing Association of the Monterey Peninsula); Tony Stott; Peter Nygaard and Grand Prix Photo; Jonathan Williams; Mike Hayward and the Mike Hayward Collection; and the John Julian Archive.

Should a reader believe that an image has been wrongly credited, please would he/she write to the publisher. A correction, if necessary, will appear in future editions of this book.

Bibliography

Anatomy of a Grand Prix Driver by Richard Garrett, Arthur Barker Ltd, 5 Winsley Street, London W1, UK (1970)

Automobile Year No. 15, 1967/1968, edited by Douglas Armstrong, Edita S.A. Lausanne, Switzerland (1967)

British Grand Prix by Maurice Hamilton, The Crowood Press, Ramsbury, Marlborough, Wiltshire SN8 2HE, UK (1989)

Can-Am Racing Cars by Karl Ludvigsen, Iconografix, PO Box 446, Hudson, Wisconsin 54016, USA (2005)

Chris Amon, Michael Clark, Celebrity Books, PO Box 302 750, North Harbour, Auckland 0751, NZ (2011)

Enzo Ferrari by Brock Yates, Doubleday, a division of Transworld Publishers Ltd, 61–63 Uxbridge Road, London W5 5SA, UK (1991)

Fast and Furious by Richard Garrett, Stanley Paul & Co Ltd, 178–202 Great Portland Street, London W1, UK (1968)

Ferrari: Men from Maranello by Anthony Pritchard, Haynes Publishing, Sparkford, Nr Yeovil, Somerset BA22 7JJ (2009)

Fifty Years of Ferrari: a Grand Prix and Sports Car racing history by Alan Henry, Haynes Publishing, Sparkford, Nr Yeovil, Somerset BA22 7JJ, UK (1997)

Forza Amon! by Eoin Young, Harper*Sports*, an imprint of HarperCollins*Publishers* (New Zealand) Ltd, PO Box 1, Auckland, NZ (2003)

Gilles Villeneuve by Gerald Donaldson, Motor Racing Publications Ltd, 46 Pitlake, Croydon CR0 3RY, UK (1989)

Grand Prix! by Mike Lang, Haynes Publishing Group, Sparkford, Yeovil, Somerset BA22 7JJ, UK (1982)

International Motor Racing Book, edited by Phil Drackett, Souvenir Press Ltd, London, UK (1967)

It Beats Working by Eoin Young, Patrick Stephens Ltd, Sparkford, Yeovil, Somerset BA22 7JJ, UK (1996)

Jim Clark at the Wheel by Jim Clark, Arthur Barker Ltd, 5 Winsley Street, London W1, UK (1964)

Motor Racing Year 1967–8, Knightsbridge Publications (1962) Ltd, West Wickham, Kent, UK (1967)

Out of the Shadows by Roger Lane, Halsgrove, Ryelands Industrial Estate, Wellington, Somerset TA21 9PZ, UK (2009)

16 On The Grid, The Anatomy of a Grand Prix by Peter Garnier, Cassell & Co Ltd, 35 Red Lion Square, London WC1, UK (1964)

Tales from the Toolbox, Michael Oliver, Veloce Publishing Ltd, Middle Farm Way, Poundbury, Dorchester, Dorset DT1 3AR, UK (2009)

The Autocourse History of the Grand Prix Car 1966–85 by Doug Nye, Hazleton Publishing, 3 Richmond Hill, Richmond, Surrey TW10 6RE, UK (1986)

The Automotive Photography of Peter Coltrin with Commentary by Phil Hill, John W. Barnes Jr. Publishing Inc. Scarsdale, New York 10583, USA (1978)

The Cruel Sport by Robert Daley, Bonanza Books, a division of Crown Publishers Inc. (1963)

The Enzo Ferrari Memoirs by Enzo Ferrari, Hamish Hamilton Ltd, 90 Great Russell Street, London WC1, UK (1963)

The Great Racing Cars and Drivers by Charles Fox, Grosset & Dunlap Inc Publishers, New York NY, USA (1972)

The Guinness Complete Grand Prix Who's Who by Steve Small, Guinness Publishing, 33 London Road, Enfield, Middlesex EN2 6DJ, UK (1994)

The Guinness Guide to Grand Prix Motor Racing by Eric Dymock, Guinness Superlatives Limited, 2 Cecil Court, London Road, Enfield, Middlesex, UK (1980)

The International Book of Grand Prix Motor Racing, edited by Michael Frewin, Leslie Frewin (Publishers) Ltd, 15 Hay's Mews, London W1, UK (1965)

The Legendary Years by Louis Stanley, Queen Anne Press, Mackerye End, Harpenden, Hertfordshire AL5 5DR, UK (1994)

The Limit, by Michael Cannell, Atlantic Books Ltd, Ormond House, 26–27 Boswell Street, London WC1N 3JZ, UK (2011)

The Monaco Grand Prix by Alex Rollo, Ian Allan Ltd, Shepperton, Surrey, UK (1987)

The Young Meteors by Jonathan Aitken, Martin Secker & Warburg Ltd, 14 Carlisle Street, London W1, UK (1967)

V65: L'efficacia di un'idea: Pubblicazzione realizzata dalla Ferrari SpA, Via Abetone Inferiore 4 – 41053 Maranello, Italy (2001)

Index

Italicised page numbers refer to illustrations.